Professional Gundog Training

Other books by Joe Irving and published by Swan Hill Press

Training Spaniels
Gundogs – Their Learning Chain

Professional Gundog Training

THE TRADE SECRETS

Joe Irving

Quiller

To my wife 'Kath' with love and appreciation for her patience in putting up with me for thirty-five years

First published in the UK in 2006
by Quiller, an imprint of Quiller Publishing Ltd
Reprinted 2008, 2011

British Library Cataloguing-in-Publication Data
A catalogue record for this book
is available from the British Library

ISBN 978 1 904057 90 1

Typeset by Phoenix Typesetting, Auldgirth, Dumfriesshire
Printed in China

Quiller

An imprint of Quiller Publishing Ltd
Wykey House, Wykey, Shrewsbury, SY4 1JA
Tel: 01939 261616 Fax: 01939 261606
E-mail: info@quillerbooks.com
Website: www.countrybooksdirect.com

Contents

Dedicated to the memory of my friend, Jack Windle, whose 'Jordieland' cockers and springers were renowned in the United Kingdom and throughout the world.

I would like to thank Edna Windle, the daughter of my old friend Jack Windle, and 'young Tom', my friend Tom Laird's son for providing me with photographs and permission to use them.

My thanks to David Hudson who supplied the bulk of the photographs.

Preface

In all of my books I have attempted to provide my readers with an innovative approach. This book is no exception. In addition to what is, I hope, a pithy treatise on the breeding and training of gundogs, I have alphabetised the entries to every aspect of dog training, for ease of quick reference. Unavoidably in employing such a format, small areas of repetition occur, but in the main this tends to emphasise the overall theme and is therefore, in my view, an advantage.

In addition to the format, for the first time ever in the gundog training book genre, I have provided my readers with a training plan, so that by being guided through their dog's training he or she will be able to curb their natural enthusiasm and by doing so, avoid the most common mistake made by the novice gundog trainer, rushing through the training at too fast a pace or putting an old head onto young shoulders.

I have also described in depth an aspect usually only briefly touched upon in most gundog books, one that appears to present the dog trainer with some difficulty, yet is in reality not as difficult or complicated as it appears: the systematic breeding of the gundog.

I would like to thank my readers who throughout the years have supported the sales of my books, and for the numerous enthusiastic accolades that I have received from them pertaining to my books.

I must confess that it was not my intention to write another book, however, I am flattered and pleased by my publisher's encouragement to do so.

It would be easy although mistaken, for the lay person to think that the working gundog world was controlled by the professional trainer. Nothing could be further from the truth. Indeed, although success in these events is required for the professional to be successful and thereby gain credence from his clients, it is much more difficult for him to do so for he has a multitude of dogs to train, whereas the amateur may only have one on which to lavish his or her full attention. It would be equally wrong to assume that because a writer contributed on a regular weekly basis to a magazine on the subject of gundog training that he was a professional trainer. As far as I am aware, until the mid 1980s, no such person other than Keith Erlandson, who contributed to the *Shooting Times*, or myself writing for the *Sporting Gun*; *Shooting News* and *Working Gundog*, ever existed. It would be understandable for the

Tom Laird, whose Criffel prefix is known throughout the world.

Jack Windle, owner of the world renowned Jordieland cocker spaniels.

uninitiated upon repeatedly seeing in the field trial results the numerous successes of a few, to assume that these were professional trainers also, when in fact they were amateur. It would be equally erroneous to assume that in this context the term 'amateur' was derogatory. Not so. Two of the most famous trainers that ever existed and who I was privileged and honoured to call my friends, Tom Laird and Jack Windle, were amateur trainers. Both were gamekeepers. Two others I knew were Danny McKenzie, a retired policeman and Bill Bremner a farmer. In fact, during the 1970s and 1980s there was, far as I am aware, only one full-time professional trainer in Scotland – yours truly.

When I published my first book, *Training Spaniels* there were very few who derived a full-time living from gundog training in the United Kingdom. It would be generous to say that there were perhaps half a dozen who could genuinely claim to be *full-time* professional gundog trainers. Until the publication of *Training Spaniels* in 1980, followed in 1983 by my second book,

Bill Bremner, a prolific collector of Scottish field trial silver in the '70s.

Gundogs – Their Learning Chain, there appeared to be a mystique held by the gundog owning public, regarding what is after all, just a semi-skilled task of training a gundog.

I confess that the deliberate attempt to explode the mystique of training the working gundog never occurred to me. However, only a few days after my first book was published, I was greeted at a field trial by a well-known amateur trainer, ex-policeman Danny McKenzie, with the remark, 'Aye – that's a fine book you've published Joe. There's only one thing wrong with it; you're telling them far too much.'

In the light of many enthusiastic compliments from amateurs and even admissions from contemporary professional trainers and writers that my books got them started, and taking into account that there are now more full-time professional gundog trainers than one could shake a stick at, then perhaps, after all, my books may have had more than a 'bit' part to play in the present ever burgeoning numbers of professional trainers.

Hopefully this will be regarded as a troubleshooting book, in that it sets out to solve the readers' gundog breeding and training problems, whilst serving as an extensive training manual in its own right.

I began training dogs in a professional capacity in 1970. During the first few years it was difficult to encourage the customers to come north of the border. It seemed somehow to be a psychological barrier. It appeared that the only dogs I seemed to get were those that had been 'started' and had developed problems. Consequently, there were times when I thought that I was running a centre for the psychologically disturbed dog, but in solving these dogs' problems, I acquired a wide and unique experience in applying psychology to dogs.

In the late 1970s, I had the idea of a Gundog Training Correspondence Course, which despite the hilarity and derisory comments it engendered from some of my contemporaries, was a resounding success. It is from this formula that the enclosed '*Macsiccar Training Plan*' was conceived. Indeed, many of my students went on to win field trials.

My proudest achievement however relates to a man, a thalidomide victim, who enquired of me if I could instruct him in training his dog because he had no arms. Not only did this man succeed, he went on to win at least one field trial.

In 1983, due to schooling problems, I gradually wound down the kennels and we moved to the urban life in Dumfries. This was, in financial terms, devastating to say the least, my only option being to return to psychiatric nursing, albeit for only a short time. As things turned out it was a wise decision.

It is understandable that a lot of friends from my training days wondered what had become of me, for despite leaving a forwarding address with the post office, we received no further mail. It is my greatest regret that I lost touch with many of them.

Not surprisingly some mystery was unintentionally generated as to my whereabouts. As late as February 2001, whilst my wife and I were on holiday in Egypt, an old military friend from Edinburgh had been enquiring in the letters' page of *The Shooting Times* if anyone could help him to find me. This of course generated even more misinformation. In spite of such misinformation, my old friend and I were reunited a short time after. Sadly, as with many of my friends, these days he is no longer with us.

Finally, to clear up the enigma: from 1983 to 1985 I returned to my old employment at Crichton Royal Hospital. From then until 2002, I rented an art studio from my brother in Dumfries, where I painted, primarily in water colours and oils, exhibited and tutored art classes. Indeed, I advertised the studio on television several times and sold my paintings, prints and my painted commemorative 'Robert Burns' plates worldwide, wherever there were ex-pat Scots. Due to a mild stroke, which rendered me partially colour blind, a heart attack, osteoporosis and chronic rheumatoid arthritis, I was compelled to retire in 2002.

As for now, I am a fanatical dry-fly angler and spend most of my time fishing, though I still miss the wee dogs, very much.

If by reading this book my readers should learn a few of the professional gundog trainers' trade secrets and are reliably guided in the training of their dogs by the 'Macsiccar Training Plan', then I will be sufficiently rewarded and the midnight oil burned in writing this book will have been justified.

Happy training.

The 'Macsiccar' Training Plan

Through the years I have often been asked what the origin of my Kennel Club prefix was. The name that I chose for my prefix, 'Macsiccar', is derived from an incident that happened in Greyfriars Church in Dumfries during the twelfth century. Robert the Bruce, then Lord of Annandale and Earl of Carrick, was informed that his cousin John the Red Comyn, Lord of Badenoch, an English knight whom he suspected of spying against him, would be worshipping in the church at a given hour. Accompanied by a henchman, the Black Douglas (it is after him that the border town Castle Douglas is named), Bruce arrived at the church and went in alone. Upon coming out, he said to his henchman, 'I have just slain the Red Comyn', to which the Black Douglas replied as he jumped from his horse, 'I'll mak sikkar' (I'll make sure). Whereupon he entered the church and stabbed the Red Comyn again. Legend has it that the Bruce and the Black Douglas then turned around the shoes on their horses, so that in the snow it would confuse their pursuers. Butch Cassidy and the Sundance Kid could have learned a thing or two from these guys.

As far as I am aware, the inclusion of a systematic training plan in a gundog training book has never been attempted before.

I am equally aware however, that by giving a concise training plan to the novice, another problem may be created. For like the trainer's eagerness to press on regardless with the dog's training, come what may, without assistance, the same eagerness may apply in his use of the plan. He may decide that, as I have provided the means whereby he can train his dog the professional way, there is no need for him to read the book. He has been provided with a short cut! This would be a grave mistake. It is vitally important that the book is read and understood, if any hope of success is to be envisaged.

My reason for including a training plan is to 'mak sikkar' that my readers will be protected from the most common mistake that the amateur trainer is liable to make – he rushes through the training at far too fast a pace, 'putting an old head onto young shoulders' as amateur trainer and writer Peter

Moxon used to say, when rushing is not at all necessary. Consequently, the novice trainer creates his own problems. It is hardly surprising then, that he convinces himself that training the dog is far too difficult after all and he doesn't have the time anyway.

It is not at all difficult and as to time, fifteen minutes per day is quite adequate.

In an effort to allay the amateur trainer's anxieties regarding the progress of his dog, which he very often mistakenly compares with a friend's dog's progress, I have indicated on the training plan a lengthier spectrum in training terms, so that the novice trainer will realise that there is no hurry and he can therefore relax. As a word of reassurance, it is not at all uncommon for some trainers to start the initial training at well over a year old. This of course is only possible with a kennel dog that has not inherited pre-training problems.

Neither should the novice trainer try to keep to the exact timing as written in the training plan. For instance, if, in the plan at the six month mark, chastisement is shown as part of Intermediate and Advanced Training; returning to the whistle during hand training is shown as part of Early and General Training; and preventing the puppy from hedgerow hunting is shown as part of General Training, it does not mean that all these aspects of training should be entered into at the same time, at the six month mark. Similarly, there is no need to worry if teaching the dog that 'Over' is to overcome an obstacle during Intermediate Training is not reached by nine months old. The idea behind the plan is that it is to be utilised as a whole, so that in time the dog may be trained successfully.

Although my motive in preparing a structured training plan is primarily to portray to the novice trainer that there is no hurry, it has to be said that there are dogs who are much quicker on the uptake than others, even within brothers and sisters of the same litter. An element of common sense decrees therefore that such dogs require to be stimulated and that too much delay in moving on can be harmful to the dog's development. I must, therefore, trust the reader to move on when, and only when, he or she is confident that the lesson has been sufficiently bedded into the dog's understanding, particularly with the dog that seems to be progressing rapidly in his initial training. There are many instances when a dog may complete his entire training with flying colours. On the other hand however, as will become progressively more apparent if one trains several dogs over the years, no two dogs are the same. Each and every one will progress and assimilate its lessons at a widely different rate in comparison to its kennel mates. The trainer must always be on guard and watchful for signs of 'burn-out' in the dog who hitherto had seemed to be progressing at an unusually rapid rate and be prepared to step back and endorse the last two or three lessons. If the regression seems very severe and the dog is displaying signs of severe 'stickiness', the trainer must be prepared to cease training for two or three lessons in order to repair the breakdown.

Months of training	The Macsiccar	
3	Hup!	Hiss!
4	E Leave it page 90	E and G Get In page 57
5	E and G Dead There page 27	E and G Gone Away page 58
6	I and A Chastisement page 17	G Hand Training page 61
7	G Get Out – Go Back page 58	G Hand Training –Sitting at Distance page 65
8	I and A Drop – Disobedience To page 33	I Over page 105
9	G Discipline page 29	I and A Quartering page 115
12	I and A Shot – Dropping to page 143	I and A Water – Introduction to page 163
14	I and A Wind Cheek Treatment page 168	I and A Wind Down Treatment page 169
16	I and A Retrieves – Frozen page 130	I and A Sheep Dogging page 143
18	I and A Unseen Multiple Dummies page 160	I and A Tracking or Taking a Line page 152
20	A Preparation for a Field Trial page 111	A Preparation for a Field Trial page 111

E = early training   G = general training

Training Plan

		Months of training
No!	E Retrieving – Encouraging a Good Delivery page 132	3
E and G Hand Training – Returning to Whistle page 66	E and G Get On page 58	4
E and I Sighted Retrieves page 145	G Association – Learning By page 2	5
G Dashing along the Hedgerows page 25	G Disobeying the 'Return' Whistle page 31	6
G Jumping page 84	G Heel page 69	7
I Discouraging Game page 30	I Hi–Lost page 72	8
I and A Quartering Cheek Wind Beat page 120	A Quartering Down Wind Beat page 123	9
I and A Water – Retrieving from page 166	G Lining Ground Scent page 93	12
A Disobedience page 31	I and A Drop – Disobedience To page 33	14
I and A The Three Ladies page 150	I and A Taking Signalled Directions at Distance page 149	16
I and A Unmarked Retrieves page 159	First Season's Experience page 46	18
A Preparation for a Field Trial page 111	A Preparation for a Field Trial page 111	20

I = intermediate training A = advanced training

Care should also be taken not to interpret the last instruction as meaning a 'quick run through' of the preceding lessons: the same time and care must be invested in the repeat lessons as though the dog was experiencing them as completely new to him. Where I hope the plan will be most successful is in illustrating to the novice trainer that, if he or she discovers that they have been mistaken and pushed on too soon, there is plenty of time available to do a short refresher.

Chapter One

A

Absconding

It seems appropriate that the 'absconding' dog should appear at the beginning of this book, for of all the problems that present themselves to the dog-owning public, this is the most common. 'He runs away and he won't come back' or 'I chased him for over two hours last night' is a familiar cry from desperate owners, when seeking help from the professional trainer. Luckily, it is also the easiest of all dog training problems to cure.

Take the dog on its lead to a wide open space where there are no other dogs or livestock. Never, ever indulge in a remedial exercise when the dog is liable to be distracted, especially by other dogs for believe me if you do, you will not stand a chance in hell! Release him and let him run off. Stand still and wait for him to stop and be assured he will, for he wishes to see how well his little game is progressing. He has discovered that if he runs off you will chase him – and it is great fun to be chased.

Once he has stopped and is looking back at you, call his name or give the recall, whatever signal that you are accustomed to give, then turn and run away from him. Initially he may just stand there staring after you, probably in disbelief and undoubtedly quite puzzled, for this is not how the game is usually played. Don't worry about this, for the first seeds of doubt have been sown in his mind. Simply stop again, repeat the recall and once more run off away from him. Eventually, even if you run out of sight of him, he will come bounding back to you. In all probability he will race past you. This is normal, for he has not given up on the idea yet that you may chase him. However, this time he will not run quite as far before he stops and looks back.

The treatment is exactly as before, give the recall and run away in the opposite direction. Before very long you will find that he will return to you whenever he is called.

Tactile praise whenever he returns is all that is then required. I do not and never have believed in giving tit-bits as a reward, except in exceptional circumstances.

Association – Learning By (General Training)

Contrary to popular belief, dogs do not understand words as such. How often have we heard an owner proudly declare, when discussing his dog's prowess, 'He knows every word I say.' This of course is just not true. It is easy and understandable for the average dog owner to fall into the trap of crediting the dog with powers which are beyond its ken. This is because we humans communicate with each other verbally and with our dogs in the same way with apparently equal success. It is perhaps not so surprising then if the average dog owner believes that because the dog is given a verbal command to which he responds appropriately, then the dog has understood the word! This of course is not the case. Words are meaningless to dogs, they are no more than sounds which, through repetitive use in conjunction with whistle sounds and reinforced with hand signals, in time become increasingly familiar to the dog which, depending on the dog's intelligence and the thoroughness of the training regime, result in the appropriate reaction. The dog accumulates knowledge by associating with the example, thereby he gains experience. If the example is a negative one, such as punishment, then the dog will react to it in a negative way. By repetitively making the same vocal sounds, very often in conjunction with the same hand signal, the dog becomes conditioned by associating and responding to the signal that he has become accustomed to.

For example, the first stage in the pup's education is when soon after they are weaned, you stand above them with a plate of food. Raising one hand with the palm facing the pups milling around your feet, you command 'Hup'. Obviously the pups do not have the slightest idea as to what this new sound is, but they smell the food and they want it, so they are excitedly falling over each other to get at it. The first time you implement this exercise you will need patience, just keep repeating 'Hup' and each time lift your hand, palm outward, towards them.

As I have said, they haven't a clue as to what this new sound is, but sooner or later the majority will sit to contemplate what is happening. Immediately put the food in front of them. The next time you stand in front of them with food and repeat the process, you will find that they stop gambolling excitedly a little sooner by sitting, whereupon put the food instantly in front of them. They have no idea what the word sound 'Hup' means but very quickly they will associate the sound with sitting, and getting the food. Ergo, they have become conditioned, in exactly the same way as Pavlov conditioned his dogs with the aid of bells. Similarly, by exhibiting the hand signal in conjunction with the word 'Hup' and their receipt of the food, you are conditioning them by association, so that in the future they will sit whenever you set the example by raising the flat hand, palm towards them. Even without the added stimuli of the 'wordsound' or the food, they will sit. In conditioning them by association in the early days of their lives, you are laying the trail for their future training: in dropping to hand, dropping to the raised gun, returning to the crouching hand-patting signal to bring the dog to hand and a plethora of other skills. Most importantly, you have taught the dog to watch your hands. Moreover you have achieved it in such a natural way that the pup will always obey the commands because as far as he can recall, it has always been this way, so disobeying the command just does not occur to him.

At this point perhaps it would be opportune for me to comment on a rather disturbing trend in dog training that has come to my attention. Many years ago there was a television dog training authority who, whenever she spoke to the dog, raised her voice into a soprano crying 'Walk-e-e-es,' or when giving praise, it was 'Good Boy-e-e-e'. In my view not only did it sound ridiculous but I felt that it was totally unnecessary. Unfortunately, this trend is now pervading the working breeds and is even used by some of our contemporary professional trainers. No doubt having been told at some time that the dog recognises your pleasure or displeasure by your tone of voice, they have mistakenly gained the impression that an exaggerated tone is required. This is not at all necessary, all that is required is your normal tone. Credit your dog with the sense to recognise whether or not you are pleased from your natural voice inflection. There is no need to treat him like a fool, so please do not patronise the dog. You should always treat him as an equal. Treat him with respect and he will respect you.

In conditioning a dog by association, we employ pleasurable stimuli, such as food or exercise. It is worth noting at this early stage of the dog's conditioning, that even food is not regarded by the dog as the most important influence in his life. Exercise is. It is of little interest to him who feeds him. He probably doesn't even notice because his eyes are on the food, but the person who exercises him is god! In my professional training days, I never allowed my kennel assistants to exercise the dogs that were in training.

Whilst this applies even with the house dog, despite all the diversionary activities that are available to him, it is of even greater importance to the dog who has no stimuli, for he is confined to a kennel and run for most of the day. It follows then that the kennel dog is less likely to present the problems that may affect the house dog. However, in recognising that the dog learns by example and association, it is crucial that we acknowledge that lack of stimulation will also have a devastating effect upon the growing puppy.

The puppy left unattended in kennels for the first three to four months of its life will be severely retarded through lack of human contact and the accompanying stimulation that this would bring to his development. There is no doubt in my mind that the dog in its wild state would learn almost all his skills from his mother.

In the kennel situation, if the trainer is the owner of the puppy's mother, then once her milk has dried up, there are great advantages to be gained by letting the pup run with his mother during exercise sessions. During the summer months, letting the pup run to the pond with his mother, means that she will be of great help to the trainer in encouraging her pup to make his first foray into the water. On the other hand the kennel dog properly attended to will also be more attentive to his trainer and we can use this to our advantage. We use pleasant stimuli, so by association the dog becomes conditioned to respond to our commands. Unfortunately, it is just as easy for the dog to be abreacted, that is, to be conditioned by unpleasant association to a devastating effect. (*see* Neurotic Aversion to Scent page 100)

Amateur Trainers

There can be little doubt that amateur trainers have enthusiasm in abundance regarding the training of their dogs. They also appear to have an insatiable appetite for knowledge but, most of all, they show an overriding eagerness to press on regardless.

Many visitors to my kennels would arrive in their car and immediately upon the pup setting foot on the ground they would command him to 'Hup!' Naturally the pup was excited and after travelling a long distance in the car, his first thought was a call of nature. The owners would get quite upset that the pup was not going to sit and they would be a little embarrassed until I told them that I would doubt the pup's intelligence if it had sat to command after such a journey.

Almost all of the puppies brought to me in those days were far too advanced for their age, old before their time. It is within this keenness, this desire to push on come what may, that the root cause of the problems that many amateur trainers encounter lies. For in their eagerness to press on, no sooner has their pupil registered that he has caught on to what is required of him regarding the lesson in hand, than the amateur goes soldiering on introducing the next step in the training far too soon. 'Make haste slowly' should be the maxim for training dogs.

The amateur trainer in the one-man-one-dog situation has a tremendous advantage over the professional trainer. The novice has only one dog to concentrate on and has much more time to lavish attention and love on his pupil. All the novice requires is advice on training and on how to be relaxed with it. Always make certain that each lesson is well and truly bedded in before you start the next progression in the training.

Chapter Two

B

Behavioural Boundaries

Behavioural patterns in the puppy, as with the child during its formative years, are strikingly similar and are directly related to the behavioural boundaries that have been laid down by the parent/teacher/trainer/handler in early life. In other words, the dog's willingness or unwillingness to comply with the trainer's commands are the end result of what limits of behaviour he has become accustomed to. It is no more complicated than that. The dog will respond to exactly what you have allowed him. It is also directly related to associated learning. The secret, if there is one, is simply consistency. Accept at all times only what you demand of him. Therein lies another danger however. In insisting on obedience from the pup or young dog, the trainer must guard against being too severe, especially with physical chastisement.

Biddability

In the gundog fraternity, it is an accepted fact that, in the main, the bitch is more amenable and thereby more easily trained than the dog. As with all manifestations in nature however, things are never as simple as that. No two bitches or dogs are alike and therefore there will always be the exception to the rule. Just as with humans there are women who are macho and men who are effeminate together with the full spectrum of individuality between. The same applies in the canine world. There is occasionally the bitch that could break the heart of a wooden god and on the other hand the dog who is gay. Nevertheless if you apply careful consideration to the personality of the breeder, by and large your speculation will result in your expectations being realised.

(Further reading: *Gundogs – Their Learning Chain*)

Boundaries v Hunting

Many years ago now, I clearly remember the end result of being too severe with earlier punishment relating to hunting boundaries that had been suffered by a young dog. I was in the line in an open qualifying stake at an estate in Yorkshire. A cock pheasant was shot, in my view, far too close to the dog at the other side of the line to be of any value as a suitable retrieve in an open stake. The bird fell two metres in front of me and approximately twelve metres to the left of his handler, a well-known trainer, who I knew very well and was familiar with his training techniques. My judge, Duggie Hurst, a part-time professional, quite rightly, asked our end of the line to step back approximately four metres. I say quite rightly, for there are many dogs that will not pick up from a stranger's feet. Indeed why should they?

The dog, an open stake winner no less (later made up to Field Trial Champion), had obviously marked the bird which was lying on a patch of open ground. Yet despite repeated vocal commands of, 'Go Back Go Back', with whistle and evermore frantic hand signals, the handler was unable, over a protracted period of time, to get his dog to go further than the area within which he had been taught to quarter when hunting. In my opinion, the dog had been physically and probably too savagely punished in relation to his quartering boundaries, to the extent that he had lost trust in his handler and the confidence to break from his accustomed hunting area for fear of further physical abuse, in spite of the added inducement of having marked the bird. I feel reasonably confident that if the bird had been shot as it departed out in front of the line, instead of out to the side. The dog would have had little difficulty in performing the retrieve, no matter how far it had fallen.

However, we go back to the dog's thinking processes. He has an excellent memory and associates the deed and the resulting punishment with the action he was involved in at the time, together with the place where he committed it. We can see why the dog could become confused, by having been punished severely in relation to his quartering parameters and then being asked to ignore the lesson and go and fetch a bird lying well outwith his normal hunting boundary. There are enough contradictions presented to the hunting dog without creating any more.

As an example, let us look at the Labrador, probably the finest retriever there is within the canine world. Now, if he is kept at heel as a no-slip retriever, he has no restrictions placed upon the area where he is required to hunt and retrieve from. His retrieving abilities are not limited in any way by his earlier training and there are no contradictions. When sent for a far distant unmarked bird, he can and does range as far as he likes and will work in response to whistle and hand directions at a great distance, for this is exactly what he was bred for. This is his forte and in my view there are few dogs to beat him in the no-slip retriever milieu.

The performance of the no-slip dog and the hunting dog's duties are widely and markedly different and it is within the varied duties expected from each that determines the easiness to train one while the other presents the most challenge to its trainer. Because of the fewer tasks required for the no-slip dog to perform, it is much easier for the trainer, even one of minimal skills to achieve success. Consequently the trainer will encounter fewer problems in the training and thereby is less likely to find that he needs to punish his pupil.

It is a fact and therefore there can be no disputing it, that training the hunting dog presents its trainer with a vastly more complex and demanding task than the training of a dog whose only duty is that he does not budge from his master's feet until he is required to retrieve. The accolade 'maid of all work' is not apportioned to the spaniel idly. On the other hand, for the handler who wishes to train his retriever to hunt and perform his duties to the same standard as the English springer or cocker spaniel, is in my view only creating problems. Horses for courses, it's as simple as that.

Due to the complexities presented in training the hunting dog, not less confusing for the dog are the many contradictions that the dog is faced with on a daily basis. Perhaps understandably then, the chances of being required to punish or merely correct the young dog are greatly increased. It is in the increased possibility for punishment wherein the trainer must tread warily, for, if too severe it will depend on the dog's temperament whether or not he will react negatively.

Let us consider what we require from the hunting dog. He must hunt his ground within the parameters of an imaginary 'box' whilst staying within shot. Upon finding the game he must flush it and not chase it, that is he must remain steady on the drop up to and after the shot until told to retrieve it or, act accordingly and carry on hunting when told 'Gone Away'. If on the other hand the shot has been successful, the dog is then required to retrieve it. If it is ground game, the dog would not be expected to need any assistance from his handler for there is the foot scent from the quarry's 'seat' to follow. If on the other hand it is a bird that is down, and quite often the dog has not marked it, then some 'sheep dogging' (handling out to the 'fall' by the handler entailing the dog's willingness to accept hand and whistle signals at distance) would be expected.

It can be seen that there are a multitude of areas in the training of the hunting dog that present contradictions which are not presented to the no-slip dog's training. Each of these contradictions are contentious areas where the trainer may be required to chastise his pupil.

The following are the areas of training not presented to the no-slip retriever. These are the daily tasks that confront the dog being trained as a hunter, excluding the pointer setter breeds, each of which may incur the displeasure of his trainer and merit correction. Firstly you are training him to sit and stay at distance. Secondly you will teach him to drop at distance to the whistle and in due course to the shot. Thirdly you will expect him to quarter i.e. hunt his ground within a box-like area always within shot. Fourthly, you will require the dog to flush the game and remain steady to it and then, perhaps the biggest contradiction of all his duties you expect him to break from steadiness and pursue and retrieve live game. A pretty tall order I think most will agree, and every facet of this training presents an area where a degree of reprimand may be required.

The psychological trainer has the insight to recognise the dog's point of view and allow for the contradictions. In this way he identifies that there are areas of training when the young dog may get confused. If for instance he sees that his pupil whilst hunting/quartering is tending to gradually take up too much ground, he will stop the dog, walk quietly up to him (never ever charge noisily up to a young dog prior to punishing him), take him by the ear, sound the turn whistle sharply in his ear whilst simultaneously giving the ear a sharp tug. This method of rebuke is a deliberate imitation of the bitch's actions with a recalcitrant pup or the action that would be taken by a dominant pack leader in the wild. It is therefore psychologically acceptable to the pup. The bitch will grasp a pup by the scruff of the neck or an ear and give it a brisk shaking. All that we have done is substitute the growl with the whistle. There will never be the remotest chance of a dog being inhibited or cowed by such methods, for he understands the treatment. The trainer who exacts extreme physical punishment on the dog who is perhaps hunting too widely or almost out of shot, may find that when he asks his dog in the future to break out of the accustomed hunting area to go for a retrieve to the left or right, outwith the imaginary box, the dog will show reluctance to do so for fear of a savage reprimand – a classic scenario where one area of the dog's education encroaches upon another negatively and which, if not dealt with properly, can have a devastating effect.

It is precisely for this reason that the hunting springer cannot be compared to the no-slip retriever in the distant retrieve. I feel that if a spaniel were to be used as a no-slip dog (although I cannot imagine why anyone would want to) taking into consideration his higher horizon because of his smaller stature, he would be just as efficient with the long range retrieve as any other no-slip dog.

If your methods are too severe in any aspect of training, you will surely pay the price. Insist on compliance with commands by all means, but with consistency, even to the point of being pedantic. However, temper your insistence with compassion. There can be no room for anything other than the mildest of physical chastisement in dog training, except for the isolated case of an extremely rumbustious character who is obviously deliberately defying his trainer. I cannot imagine a lion tamer getting into the cage and giving one of his pupils a punch on the ear. Can you? (*see* Association – Learning By page 2; Chastisement page 17; Case Hardening page 16)

Blinking Game

There is a very distinct difference between 'missing' and 'blinking' game. If a dog hunts its ground and passes over game without acknowledging its presence, that dog can be accused of 'missing' game and it would be fair to say that its scenting abilities are suspect. On the other hand, if a dog alters his hunting pattern and homes in on one spot indicating excited body language, then passes on without flushing the game which thereafter makes its presence known, that dog can be accused of 'blinking' the game. Both are eliminating faults in a field trial.

Blood Scent v Powder Scent

Until I wrote my first book *Training Spaniels* in 1980, the sporting fraternity held the view that dogs taking a line to wounded game were following a 'blood scent'. I never accepted this, for how often upon retrieving a wounded bird is it seen to be bleeding to any noticeable degree? I have on more than one occasion had a rabbit retrieved showing only signs of shot in the head and ears but no blood, yet the dog had followed the line without deviating from it in spite of unwounded rabbits getting up in his path and making their escape, it seems reasonable to assume that it must be another very recognisable scent that allows the dog to differentiate between shot and unshot game amidst an abundance of foot and body scents. In the case of birds, we have all seen on many occasions a dog following a runner unerringly, whilst at the same time flushing birds along the way which he totally ignored. Clearly then the dog recognises some appreciable difference between the shot bird, as opposed to the unshot bird.

One April morning I was giving a young dog some shooting over rabbits. There had been a light shower of rain a few moments earlier and the sun had just reappeared. Scenting was just about as good as it gets. The dog flushed a rabbit from its seat and I shot it. Immediately upon the shot hitting the ground, I noticed a very distinct line of vapour from the wet grass leading up to the dead rabbit. As the dog was sitting steadily and had obviously marked the rabbit, I decided that the retrieve would be too easy for him and therefore I walked forward to pick up the rabbit by hand.

Upon reaching down I was struck by the very distinct and unmistakable odour of gunpowder rising from the wet grass. It is widely believed that a dog's scenting capabilities are around fifty times that of humans. I am not so sure that its scenting capabilities could be so precisely quantified, however, there can be no argument that the canine olfactory propensities are vastly greater than ours. It begs the question then, if I could smell the powder scent, how much more distinct must it be to the dog? I suggest that we could liken the powder scent trail left by a wounded bird or rabbit, as distinct to the dog as a motorway is to us. I put it to my readers therefore that albeit purely by chance, I have solved the controversial question of 'blood scent'. The dogs were working on powder scent.

Boredom

This is usually initiated unintentionally by the amateur trainer. It is often the end result of too much repetition of a particular aspect of training. For instance, a frequent complaint is the refusal to retrieve, commonly the result of the children's game of throwing endless uninteresting objects for the pup to retrieve especially when Dad is at work. Dad of course does not escape blame either, for how many amateur trainers will admit to the fact that every time they throw a dummy the dog is asked to retrieve it?

Boredom may also be caused by the training session being too lengthy. The novice trainer commonly holds the belief that two lengthy training sessions at the weekend will redress the daily training balance that the young dog should be receiving. This is most definitely not the case. The longer training session is not at all advantageous for either the dog or his trainer. It is essential that the training bouts should be short and regular, thereby keeping the dog interested and enthusiastic. Moreover, it is of the utmost importance that the exercises should always end on a successful note. It is said, 'never let the sun set on an argument'. The same dictum applies equally with your dogs. If the training exercises are too lengthy, there is the very real danger of the pup losing interest altogether and becoming progressively more and more disobedient. Therefore if you persist, you will most certainly court disaster with frustration and exasperation leading to anger and the whole exercise ending in failure.

Dogs that present the amateur trainer with such problems would be brought to me for canine psychiatric treatment. The owner, when asked, would reiterate his tale of woe and despondency. On being informed that he should keep the training sessions short and frequent in order to keep the dog interested, the reply would be, 'Oh! but during the week because of work, I just don't have the time.' My comment on hearing this excuse would run along the lines of, 'Who exercises him during the week?' If, as was very often the case, the customer replied, 'I do', my answer usually surprised them, for I would tell him, 'Then you have all the time in the world necessary to train him.' Ten minutes training per day will cultivate success much more readily than two hours on Sunday.

Boredom displayed by their dog is not only a problem for the amateur. The professional's dogs can also be victims of boredom for a variety of reasons – kennel sickness (which can be likened to reactive depression in the human) being one. However the professional has the advantage or he should have, of knowing what to do about it.

Advice

It is essential that in these cases 'training' as such must be delayed for the time being. Beyond all else, the 'bounce' must be put back into the dog. He must show that he is enjoying life again. If the dog is refusing to retrieve, then, for the time being, a short holiday from retrieving will do no harm and will probably do a power of good. The same applies to any particular aspect of training. Simply keep him occupied with other little training exercises for the moment. If at the end of this respite he still refuses to retrieve, then you may have to decide on a course of forced retrieving. If the dog is refusing to hunt, then again you must put the bounce back into him. It has to be said, a puppy must under no circumstances be left neglected in a kennel. A special effort must be made to humanise him: take him out frequently; talk to him; get the children to play with him (properly informed children are probably the best humanisers there are); and generally whenever you are near his kennel, make the effort to speak to him in passing. Irreversible damage will ensue if a pup, just as with a child, does not receive sufficient human contact in its early months. It will damage them for the rest of their life.

(*see* Association – Learning By page 2; Retrieving – Forced page 137)

Breakers

In my view there can never be any excuse for the treatment dealt out to the dog by the breaker's odious methods. Thankfully, due no doubt to a more enlightened training fraternity, the numbers of breakers appear to be diminishing now. Simply put, the breaker will run a dog from the time when it is a pup through to, in some cases, as late as eighteen months old, very often in a group. I have known those who didn't even bother to name the dogs until such times as they were ready for 'training'.

Until the time that the breaker deemed them ready for breaking, very few, if any commands were given. The dogs were simply allowed to range over the hills, chasing rabbits in the pack situation. Needless to say these dogs having been allowed unbridled freedom, became very enthusiastic and efficient hunters. Thereafter, once the so-called training commenced, they were beaten into submission in order to comply with the breaker's wishes. Suffice it to say, the wastage caused by such methods is extreme, for only the toughest of dogs survive such treatment. A dog should be trained in such a way that he will work for you, because you are his god and he wants to please you, not because he is afraid of what you will do to him. On occasion however, 'free hunting' can be utilised to our advantage.

(*see* Association – Learning By page 2; Neurotic Aversion to Scent page 100; Case Hardening page 16)

Breaking Cover

This is when, after hunting in thick undergrowth and flushing game, an experienced dog will hustle ground game out to the edge of the cover then stop and remain steady, watching to mark the game if shot. Some will remain standing yet perfectly steady, others will sit or lie down immediately after breaking from the cover. I have no objection to the dog who does this provided it is within reason, that is, the 'find' is perhaps two or three metres from the edge of the cover.

However, it could be fairly argued, and entirely within the judges' discretion, that moving after the flush is admittedly a fine line, a grey area, an honest fault if there can be such a thing, between the dog's desire to mark the game and an indication of being unsteady to the flush of game. Ever mindful of the fact that the prime purpose of the hunting gundog is to find game for the gun, and fill the bag, I would value such an intelligent animal very highly indeed for rough shooting purposes, for he is illustrating that he has acquired 'game sense'. He knows what his job is and has broken cover merely to sight the game; in other words, he is working as a team with his handler and the guns. He has learned the killing power of the gun. Such a dog is a gem beyond price and a bonus to any shoot. However, knowing that it is a grey area I would have to exercise circumspection as to the wisdom of competing with such a dog in a trial.

Breeder

The prospective gundog owner could be excused for believing that there could be little contention involved in purchasing a puppy. The potential risk is one that very few contemplating buying a pup would ever even think of – it is not to consider the character of the breeder. Each breeder or trainer selects the sires for his bitches very carefully indeed. He knows from many years of experience what he is looking for and he will select the sire from whom he expects to get the kind of progeny with which he has enjoyed most success in training and field trials.

If he appears to you to be a rather tough and rough-looking character, then unless you have a similar personality you would be well advised to exercise some careful consideration before purchasing a pup from him. The pups that he breeds will reflect his personality. They will be inherently tough enough to stand the treatment that such trainers are liable to mete out to them. The novice trainer would do well to think twice before purchasing such pups, for, unless he feels confident that he could train a dog with such boisterous and possibly belligerent disposition, he may well find that the task is too much for his inexperienced hands and discover too late that the dog has trained him. On the other hand, the same can be said of the breeder who appears to be a kindly person, for he too will breed the dogs with which he has experienced the most success through the years, therefore his pups are liable to be of a more kindly and malleable spirit. The risk in this instance being, if you tend to be of rather a forceful, impatient or short-tempered nature, then you would be wise to avoid such puppies, for they are most unlikely to blossom in your care.

What puppy to choose? Well, how long is a piece of string? There seems to be an ever confusing array of advice for the prospective buyer. My personal preference is to avoid the pup with a pale or bluish-tinged eye, because it will likely manifest itself in maturity as a yellow 'hard' eye. The bearer of such eyes, can turn out to be unstable and very often untrainable. I like a nice dark eye well-spaced in a good head. I do not hold fully to the notion that a shy puppy is necessarily a dud. This is from personal experience. One busy Sunday in 1975, Stan Lewis, a well-known amateur trainer from Cheshire, turned up at my kennels and offered to sell me one of two pups of eight weeks old, by F.T.Ch. Rivington Santa Claus out of

Lewstan Busy. The dog was quite a bold little character and of course I chose him, for the little bitch was cowering away in a corner. But after a short time, I decided to buy both pups from Stan, for one hundred and fifty pounds for the pair. In the fullness of time the dog turned out to be a fairly proficient shooting dog. What of the little bitch? From the very first I had a growing feeling that I had accidentally stumbled on to something very special, and I named her Macsiccar Michele. I hasten to add though that, in the main, the advice to pick what you think is the boldest pup is sound. My advice would be watch them in the group with their brothers and sisters and take the one who seems to be coming out on top in the general mêlée.

Breeding

It goes without saying that the bitch owner will consider the choice of sire to be of paramount importance in order to maintain the standards of quality from the bitch's litter.

Due to man's intervention in the breeding of animals, the theme pertaining to the survival of the fittest no longer applies. There are dogs used at stud today that would, in the normal pack environment, never have had the opportunity to mate and thereby perpetuate his ilk due to his lowly status. Indeed, there are dogs so effeminate that they would have been cast out of the pack to fend for themselves, and as wild dogs and wolves are pack hunters, left alone such dogs would swiftly perish in the wilderness.

However, as the Bard wrote, 'The best laid plans of mice and men oft go agley' and the breeding of dogs is no exception. Due to the whimsies of Mother Nature, the resulting litter may not come up to the expectations of the breeder. Even though the breeder carefully chose what he or she thought was a strong sire, it is not unusual to find one or two of the offspring to be of a very soft disposition. From the training point of view, this need not be a disaster, for such dogs are a boon to the novice handler insofar as they are usually of superior intelligence with a kindly nature and will never challenge their trainer.

'Timidity' is an inherent fault, however, and as such is the end result of a double-recessive gene, one recessive gene from each parent's chromosome. The single recessive gene is subservient and is masked by the dominant gene until such circumstances arise that due to a familial linked pairing it draws strength from its link to influence inherent characteristics in the progeny. Due to the single recessive gene being masked, it may lie dormant, undetected for many generations before making its presence known.

On the other hand the union between the strong sire and a 'macho' bitch, may produce in the offspring a couple of dogs that are 'too hot to handle' who will always query who is the boss by continually challenging their trainer. Such dogs are the Alpha males and will probably be untrainable in the novice trainer's hands. Of high intelligence, this is the dog who may compete with some minor success in his first few trials, but gradually increasingly demonstrate behaviour in a trial that he never displays at any other time. The field trial fraternity recognise this as 'trial minded'. Usually great performers, such dogs' trial careers are sadly of short duration and they are either sold off, or relegated to life in kennel. Macsiccar Cherokee, a magnificent specimen of his breed, was one put to stud, and many of his descendants achieved Field Trial Championship.

It can be seen therefore that breeding dogs, even those of a high order, is by no means cut and dried, and requires much speculation from the bitch owner before choosing a sire.

A word of warning would not go amiss here. Upon arriving at the stud dog's kennels, it is by no means unusual for a 'busy' stud dog to be somewhat less than enthusiastic on your bitch. It does not happen often, but there might be the unscrupulous breeder out there who upon noting the situation will suggest to the bitch owner, that his bitch is not 'quite ready' yet, but if the bitch owner will leave the bitch overnight the problem will be solved in the morning. Without resorting to Deoxyribonucleic Acid Testing, (DNA), which is far too expensive, the bitch owner has no proof that the chosen stud was used on his bitch. Better to be safe than sorry and take the bitch away. You must always see the deed done, it's as simple as that.

Macsiccar Cherokee.

Chapter Three

C

Car Sickness

After 'absconding' this is probably the most common complaint made by owners. Just as there are humans who are poor travellers through genetical inheritance, so it is with dogs and then there is little other than dosing with some medications that can be done about it. Most dogs who are poor travellers are the result of having been introduced to the car too late and as soon as practicable, the puppy should be taken on several short car trips over a period of a few weeks.

Advice

Obviously it is required that the dog learns to associate the car with a pleasurable experience. Therefore, instead of feeding the dog indoors or in his kennel, you must put him into the car with his dinner. For the first few days, leave the door ajar, then for the following three to four days shut the car door and wait until he has finished his meal. Each time he has obviously finished his dinner, remove him immediately from the car and make a great fuss of him.

The next step is to put him in the car as usual with his food, close the car door and start the engine. Watch his reaction. If he exhibits signs of wariness or distress, reverse the procedure by returning to the normal routine of feeding him in the car but without starting the engine for a few days, then try him with the engine running again. Unless his car sickness is genetic, in which case we know that only medication will succeed, you should note a gradual diminishing of his uneasiness until he doesn't take any notice of the engine whatsoever. The next stage is to put him in the car and take him for a short trip. All being well you should increase the distance each day. Consequently, by association, the dog has learned by the pleasurable example and thereby we have conditioned him.

Under no circumstances should a dog be fed before travelling.

Case Hardening

There are dogs that are so naturally defiant where the natural progression through nagging to punishment thereby developing into case hardening in the normal sense, just does not apply. These are the dogs that are generally highly intelligent and in the pack environment would probably be the pack leader. Such dogs will constantly challenge their trainers, to the extent that they may even be untrainable. Occasionally, although not commonly for generally gundogs tend to be of a tender loving nature, such dogs are capable of biting their trainer.

In the normal sense, case hardening is a matter of development, initially brought about by the trainer constantly nagging the dog and through time becoming so exasperated that he commences physical correction. It happens exactly the same way with children if the mother is forever nagging and verbally abusing, threatening and reprimanding the child, and at times even endorsing the rebuke by giving the mischievous child the occasional slap. In the absence of consistency and as children are supreme optimists in time they will expect that nothing will come of the reprimand and totally ignore, even defy her. The same applies to the henpecked husband who has learned to ignore the constant nagging even to the point of not hearing his wife.

So it is with dogs. If you are continually giving orders, chattering away at the dog he will soon learn to ignore you. This in turn will lead to the dog disobeying commands. The ever-increasing belligerence by the dog will result in the dog receiving physical correction undoubtedly through frustration on the part of the handler. Initially the punishment will tend not to be too severe but in time will gradually increase in severity until the dog has built up resentment and loss of trust in his trainer. Finally the dog will develop increasing resistance to the physical beatings. Depending on their temperament some dogs will become cowed by the savagery of the treatment, whilst others will defy the trainer and thereby become case hardened.

Advice

It seems obvious we just do not let this scenario develop in the first place. When you are handling or training a dog you must keep the word sounds to a minimum and furthermore make every sound mean something. Do not forget that if you are constantly chattering to a friend the dog does not know the difference. Never place yourself in the position where if you give a command, the dog may disobey it. Remember, consistency is the key to training dogs. Keep the sessions short and frequent, the commands as few and as quiet as possible, but insist on obedience. In this way, you have always got something in reserve inasmuch as if you raise your voice, the dog will instantly take note of it, but it must be kept as the last resort if it is to convey any emphasis. Always end a training session on a positive note by giving the dog something easy to do and thereby creating the opportunity of praising him. Enlightened by the knowledge that dogs associate their deeds with the

amazon.co.uk

Thank you for shopping at Amazon.co.uk!

Invoice for
Your order of 12 July, 2012
Order ID 203-2467642-5167563
Invoice number D2ZQqcGZN
Invoice date 13 July, 2012

Billing Address
Allan Fowler
2, Buckingham Way
Sawtry
Huntingdon, Cambridgeshire PE28 5NF
United Kingdom

Shipping Address
Allan Fowler
2 Buckingham Way
Sawtry
HUNTINGDON, Cambs PE28 5NF
United Kingdom

Qty.	Item	Our Price (excl. VAT)	VAT Rate	Total Price
1	**Professional Gundog Training: The Trade Secrets** Hardcover. Irving, Joe. 190405790X (** P-1-A100H170 **)	£13.96	0%	£13.96
	Shipping charges	£0.00		£0.00
	Subtotal (excl. VAT) 0%			£13.96
	Total VAT			£0.00
	Total			£13.96

Conversion rate - £1.00 : EUR 1,27

This shipment completes your order.

You can always check the status of your orders or change your account details from the "Your Account" link at the top of each page on our site.

Thinking of returning an item? PLEASE USE OUR ON-LINE RETURNS SUPPORT CENTRE.

Our Returns Support Centre (www.amazon.co.uk/returns-support) will guide you through our Returns Policy and provide you with a printable personalised return label. Please have your order number ready (you can find it next to your order summary, above). Our Returns Policy does not affect your statutory rights.

Amazon EU S.a.r.L, 5 Rue Plaetis, L-2338, Luxembourg
VAT number : GB727255821

Please note - this is not a returns address - for returns - please see above for details of our online returns centre

717/DFZlqcGZN/-1 of 1-//1M/econ-uk/6267812/0714-13:00/0713-17:18 Pack Type : C3

spot where they were committed and equally the correction, we are forewarned and thereby forearmed. Bearing in mind that dogs have a long memory and are acutely aware of areas where they have committed a felony and been reprimanded, it is best to avoid that particular area for the next week or so. Heaven forbid that you have resorted to physical chastisement, but if you have then this warning is doubly important.

Advice

The message I am trying to impart is, speak quietly at all times in the company of your dogs, reserve the raised tone only for emergencies when it will register with the dog as an important order. If you cultivate an air of mystery with your dog by never doing the expected or following the same pattern each day and always finish the day on a successful note, the dog will look upon you as the most important thing in his life. He will then learn to be attentive to your every move, even though it may not appear so.

Chastisement (Intermediate & Advanced Training)

Within the general dog-owning public, undoubtedly chastisement is the most emotive and contentious issue regarding training. It is probably due to this, that many authors appear to avoid it like the plague. We gundog trainers must be aware that it is essential when establishing our early relationship with the dog to tread warily when considering punishment, because whether we eventually succeed or suffer failure depends upon our actions at this crucial time. It is in these early months, when the dog learns his trust or distrust of his owner and when he will grow to like or dislike you. If treated correctly he will become devoted to you, if treated unjustly he will become distrustful, wary and reluctant to perform even the simplest of tasks. In short all will depend on the rapport acquired between the dog and his trainer at the beginning of their relationship.

Advice

From the outset, start as you mean to go on. Do not nag the dog, avoid giving unnecessary commands just for the sake of it. It is worth considering that every time you give a command it affords the dog the opportunity to disobey it. Make as few demands upon him as possible and when you do, as far as is practicable, speak to him quietly. However if you have given a command that you know he understands because he has complied with it in the past, you must insist on it being obeyed.

Punishment in the first six months of the puppy's life should not be uppermost in the trainer's mind. Thereafter physical punishment in the dog's future life should be as surgery is to medicine, very much the last resort. The only reprimand necessary in correcting a pup should consist of no more than a gruff vocal rebuke accompanied occasionally by a sharp shake of the scruff of his neck. A dog does not understand violence, nevertheless if physical punishment is administered in moderation, providing it is given on the exact spot where the dog had committed the offence, it may have the desired effect. It is vitally important that the dog trainer understands the psychology of his canine pupil.

Ask yourself, have you ever seen a bitch chastise her pup by giving him a swift clout on the ear? Of course you haven't, that is a ridiculous concept. However, I warrant that she can exercise a control over her pups far greater than any trainer. The pups understand completely their behavioural boundaries within the litter environment and what their mother expects of them.

Far too many dogs through the ages have been needlessly cowed by being physically beaten. We know that the dog associates his deeds with the spot where he has committed them. Therein lies the greatest of all secrets in the training of dogs, for we use this knowledge, coupled with consistency to our advantage. In the course of training your dog, except in exceptional circumstances, we will apply only the restraints upon the dog that his mother would

He must be taken back to where he committed the offence and rebuked on that exact spot.

use. Applied correctly and with consistency there will never be the slightest danger of your dog becoming cowed or fearful of you. He will recognise and accept his correction pertaining to the exact spot where he committed his misdemeanour.

The classic example in most books is quite rightly, the dog 'running in' and chasing the rabbit. Providing the dog was experienced and therefore fully aware that he should have stopped upon flushing the rabbit, my solution was always to take off my cap and chuck it onto the exact spot from where the rabbit was flushed, then I was off in hot pursuit of the dog. (I was a lot younger and fitter then!) Once caught, I would take him by the scruff of the neck, lifting his forepaws from the ground and without uttering a word to him I would take him back to my cap. On that spot he would reap his reward. I would flap back his ear and blast the stop whistle three or four times, simultaneously repeatedly pushing his nose into the rabbit's seat. This whistle command would be interspersed with the vocal command 'Dead – There; Dead – There'. I would then leave him sitting and back off, never taking my eye from him, whilst gruffly ordering him 'Hup–hup!'

An alternative milder rebuke is, once you have taken him back to the spot where he had flushed the rabbit, as before, you blast the stop whistle signal whilst grasping him on both sides of his cheeks just below his ears, shake him vigorously and staring into his eyes, growl, 'There–There–Hup–Hup!'

I have never known a dog who resented this treatment or showed any ill effects from it. Always when restarting the dog hunting after having been

Chastisement.

rebuked for running in, it is most important to cast him off in the opposite direction to that which the rabbit had taken, and insist that he obeys. With consistency, their steadiness to game invariably improved. Be pedantic if necessary. Consistency in all aspects of training is the key. Never be lazy. If he commits a felony do not under any circumstance let him get away with it. Herein lies a danger however, you must never under any circumstance chastise or punish a dog unless you are sure that the misdemeanour is not the result of confusion, nor whilst the dog has an object in his mouth. Counting ten before deciding to administer any form of correction is a good idea. Try not to look into a dog's eyes if he is approaching you for they don't like it and if you think about it, the eye to eye confrontation between dogs is recognised as a hostile challenge.

'Act in haste, repent at leisure' is an excellent maxim.

(*see* Association – Learning By page 2; Behavioural Boundaries page 5; Case Hardening page 16)

Check Cords

There are trainers who will use this gadget extensively. I have never been numbered amongst them, for as far as I was concerned this paraphernalia represented nothing more than an absolute nuisance, for it would snag on any tussock of grass, twig, dock leaf etc. In my view the advantages, if any, received by using this device are distinctly debatable. These days they are manufactured to a very high degree of excellence, consisting of a long flat and very strong retractable nylon tape housed in a neat plastic handle with

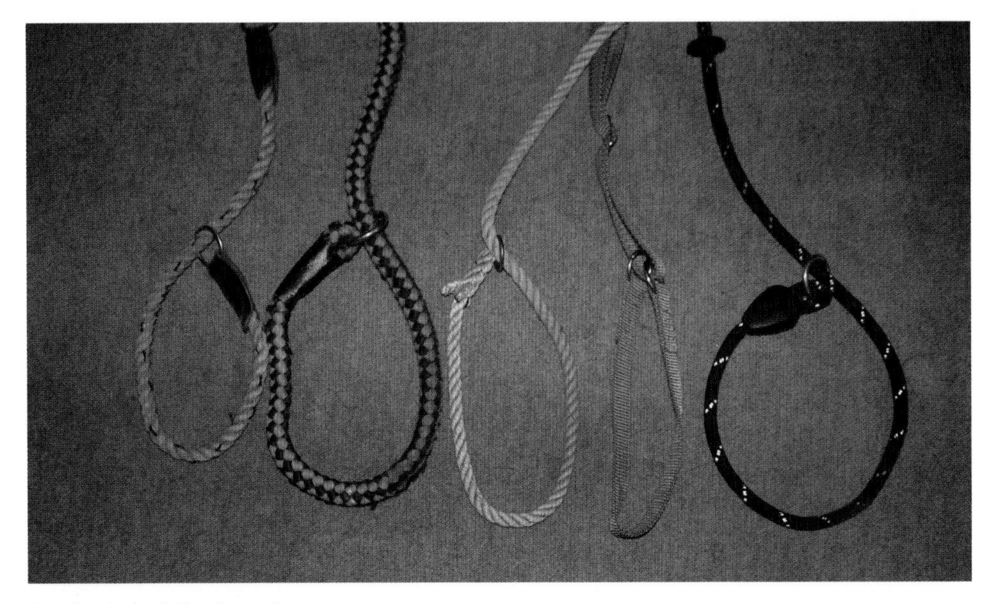

A selection of check cords.

a trigger, which allows the dog to run out to the limit of the tape. In days gone by we made our own, usually very crudely and out of string or baling twine. It is worth remembering that the modern retractable leads have been styled from the gundog check cord of old and have been adapted to suit the household pet whilst it is out for a walk. In the training of the gundog the intention is to keep the dog in check whilst quartering its ground, and in the final analysis to check the dog and hold it steady to flushed game. In my view it is doubtful if the check cord ever results in any appreciable degree of success, for I credit the dog with the intelligence to know the difference between being tethered by the neck and running free.

It is entirely the trainer's prerogative as to whether he uses this tool or not. In my view, it is of little value other than in the early training of a pointer, to encourage a young dog who is reluctant to deliver to hand, or, to assist a water-shy pup to enter water for the first time.

Conditioned Experience

It is important that the gundog owner, if he wishes to stand even the remotest chance of success in training, should understand how his dog thinks. The dog does not have the power of imagination. He cannot contemplate committing an action and visualise the repercussions likely to evolve from it. However, it would not be too difficult for the amateur trainer to believe that his dog was using imagination, for instance in dropping to shot or game in the knowledge that if he didn't he would be rebuked. That is not imagination per se, it is the result of the conditioning experience in his earlier training.

The inability to imagine is classically illustrated by a young dog I had in training many years ago in my early days as a professional trainer, who, in the final stages of his education performed every manoeuvre in his training perfectly; there was only one snag, he did everything in slow motion. I was at my wits' end, yet I had to do something, for time was running short and a client will only pay the bills for so long.

I pondered on this phenomenon as I went home that evening, then it dawned on me: perhaps the dog was slow because the whole process was just routine to him. He would hunt as he had been taught to do, a shot would be fired and he would drop, a few moments later to be sent for a fur-skinned dummy. Just lately nothing seemed to have changed as far as he was concerned. He would hunt in the thick bracken, there would be an increasingly interesting scent then, suddenly a brief glimpse of a shape that would instantly disappear, then a stop whistle, a shot would be fired and he would be required to go through the same old routine, to be sent for the retrieve which was slightly different from what he had been used to, for it seemed softer and had that exciting smell about it.

The next evening I was hunting him in the thick bracken (if you could call it 'hunting' for as usual he was painfully slow). Acting on a hunch, I decided to coax him over to the edge of the bracken and hunt the few outlying clumps in the hope that a rabbit might bolt out into the open. In no time at all a rabbit broke from the edge of the bracken right in front of him and ran across a clearing. He had stopped and could see the rabbit as it tumbled to my shot. Having waited for a suitable interval I sent him for it, half expecting the usual slow response. Immediately I noticed that for the first time in training he had raised a gallop, picked the rabbit and ran back to deliver it in fine style. Upon my giving him the 'Get On' signal again, I was astonished, for he was hunting so fast I could hardly control him.

My mistake was that I had not taken into account that every dog will slow down as their training progresses, depending on the individual dog's temperament. This is due to a combination of circumstances, preoccupation with your commands together with a degree of uncertainty. An excellent yardstick from which to envisage the dog's potential, whilst he has slowed during training, is to recollect how fast or how slow he was as an uninhibited pup before any demands were put upon him. It is a fair bet that the speed of that particular pup will return once the dog is fully trained and has renewed his confidence. It occurred to me that the dog was slow as a result perhaps of my over-training him, therefore he was lacking in confidence, preoccupied with the task in hand and not impossibly – bored!

That evening, for the first time in his life, he had flushed a rabbit at the edge of the cover and had seen the rabbit topple to the shot. It was the dawn of his realisation. At last he had learned the killing power of the gun. The 'penny' had dropped: he now knew what his purpose was and he would never be slow again.

Creative Imagination

Many years ago I sent a dog after a bird which had run into the woods. There was a wire mesh fence topped with one strand of barbed wire skirting the wood. I heard him yelp as he jumped over it, then he was gone in pursuit of the runner. A few minutes later I spied him running up and down behind the fence with the bird in his mouth looking for an exit. As I approached to help him I noticed that he seemed to be trailing something behind him. To my horror I realised that it was his entrails covered with pine needles and other fragments of vegetation.

I must confess that at this awful revelation I panicked. Hurriedly I replaced the intestines as best I could and wrapping the dog in my scarf, I was off to the nearest vet, post haste. The vet after assessing the situation and noting my obvious anxiety quickly reassured me. He informed me that there was nothing to worry about, that the wound which stretched from the dog's sternum bone almost to his crotch was superficial, all it required was cleaning plus sutures. Whilst he performed the treatment, my dog lay on his back on the table wagging his tail. I remarked upon this and was told that if it were one of us, at the very least we would be suffering great traumatic shock, for we would imagine all sorts of horrors, even visualise the possibility of death. However as it was a dog it could not visualise the possible results, imaginary or otherwise.

I would not, under any circumstances, advocate that such an operation be performed on a DIY basis, on the shooting field, or, anywhere else for that matter. I could not blame my reader if he was to think that no right-minded person would. By the strangest quirk of coincidences, it was only a few weeks after writing about the past incident, that I received a 'phone call from an old friend, a field trial competitor. In the general context of our conversation, bearing in mind that I had not disclosed that I was writing another book, he related the following tale, notwithstanding that it is hearsay, I have no reason to doubt its veracity.

In general conversation with a local gamekeeper, a former colleague of his in the south-west of Scotland, he was told of the following incident. Another 'famous trainer', who regularly rents rabbit shooting in this area, in order to prepare his dogs for the trials, sent his dog over a barbed wire fence, and, my reader has guessed the rest. Upon the dog returning with most of its entrails dragging behind it, the gamekeeper, rightly so, suggested taking the dog to the local vet. The handler refused, saying that he had some fishing nylon in his car. With the aid of the gamekeeper albeit reluctantly holding the dog down, without a local anaesthetic, the trainer stitched up the dog's wound. Should any of my readers at any time witness an act of cruelty, there is only one action that can be taken with a clear conscience – report it immediately to the police. Also, a word of warning, do not, under any circumstances, leave your dog with a professional trainer, without visiting it regularly.

Advice

This incident taught me a valuable lesson. Never again would I send a dog over a barbed wire fence. Even in field trials when presented with a retrieve which entailed the dog having to jump a barbed wire fence, or any obstacle, I would always request that I was allowed to lift the dog over such an obstruction. There is no doubt that it looks much more stylish if the dog jumps such impediments. Nevertheless, if you think anything of your dog you are well advised to avoid the danger. As far as field trials are concerned you are entitled to request that you aid the dog over any such obstacle (*see* Kennel Club Field Trial regulations Annex B. Guide to the conduct of field trials, 'Judging' section F.) and I would seriously advise my readers never to ask a dog to jump over a barbed wire fence, or, any obstacle into unseen territory.

As I have said, it taught me a valuable lesson, from then on I trained all my dogs to sit automatically upon coming up to a fence or a drystone wall and wait for orders, then when ordered over or helped, to sit again on the other side until ordered to get on. I once saw a dog launch itself over a drystone wall only to be found a few minutes later dead, impaled on farm machinery that had been parked behind the wall. The gift of imagination leads to our incredible inventiveness and is probably the greatest difference in thinking between man and the animal.

Crowd Shyness

In the family environment I would find it most unusual for this complaint to manifest itself. I would think that if it did, it would most likely be in an animal so mentally disturbed as to be virtually untrainable. However, on the other hand, if the owner was perhaps an amateur trainer who was 'over-dogged', not at all an unusual scenario, then there could be a pup, left for lengthy periods of time in kennel without enough humanising, who would manifest this complaint.

Advice

If noticed in time the treatment is obvious – humanisation. If you have children then let the pup play with them, but warn them not to throw balls for him. Children are great 'humanisers'. Once some improvement has been noticed regarding the pup's attitude to the children, it is time for socialising him in town, but keep him on the lead at all times. It seems that it is not generally known, but it is against the law to be in charge of a dog which is untethered in built-up areas. Stand for a little while here and there, wherever there is lots of pedestrian traffic. If one of the passing members of the public wishes to stroke him, then this is all to the good. Take him into a pub, anywhere where he will get the opportunity to meet people, not for too long initially, but increasing the period as time goes by. Lastly, take him in the car with you as often as possible.

Chapter Four

D

Dangerous Venues

It would seem that little attention, if any, is paid by the novice trainer regarding his surroundings when considering giving a training lesson to his dog. Yet if success is to be hoped for, a little thought would not go amiss. Without doubt it is very important for the trainer to be aware of the surroundings regarding each training venue and the possible effects that they may have on his pupil, before attempting any educational regime. During the various hand training lessons, it is most important that there are as few distractions as possible within the area. It can be most frustrating trying to maintain a young dog's attention when he is more interested in investigating that enticing scent nearby. Ideally the place to instruct the dog in hand training is on land that has little or no scent upon it, in other words, on land that is as barren as possible. Above all else, the dog should never be allowed to see the rabbit until such times as he has demonstrated that he is one hundred per cent rock steady to the 'thunderer' stop whistle signal.

It may seem to be stating the obvious when saying that no-one would be silly enough to attempt to train his dog in the middle of a field of livestock such as sheep, cows, bullocks or where horses were grazing! Farm creatures tend to be rather curious and at the first sight of a dog will crowd in upon it. Obviously from then on any training would be a non-starter. Surprising though it may seem, I have on many occasions observed just such a scenario.

Dashing along the Hedgerows (General Training)

The term livestock where gundog training is concerned could be interpreted as any living creature liable to have an effect on the dog's education. The enlightened trainer will take into account every possible eventuality when considering a training site. In training the gundog, one of the most hazardous, albeit innocent-looking locations where the trainer can be caught unawares is, believe it or not, when allowing the pup to scamper in and out of the hedgerows at either side of a country lane. For the novice trainer it would be easy not to notice, or even to attach any importance to it if he did,

Two examples of dangerous training grounds because of poor visibility.

that the pup is boring away out ahead, chasing flocks of small birds. However it would be foolish to ignore this, for if the pup gets into the habit of pulling away out to forty, fifty or more metres in front of you, it would be surprising if difficulties were not encountered in his future training, especially in keeping him within shot. In addition to this, allowing a young dog to chase small birds is also liable to create the wrong impression in the future when you ask him to remain steady to game.

Whilst any problem stemming from hedgerow hunting can by no means be construed as insurmountable, why make life difficult? Isn't it more sensible to avoid the problem being created in the first place? For the same reasons, never allow a young dog to go chasing after any birds that may be congregated in the middle of a field.

Advice

When walking a young dog down a country lane, be watchful and alert to what is going on. A good trainer will always capitalise on the surroundings by using them to his advantage, and using the terrain with a mind to the dog's future training. Therefore, as soon as you notice that the dog is getting too far ahead of you, call him back by using the return whistle signal and, crouching down with a simulated 'patting' motion of the hand, point him into the hedge again at your feet. Just keep repeating this every time he appears to be getting too far down the hedge from you, approximately three to four metres in front is sufficient. By doing this you are training him without his being aware of it.

This is the method of 'training' that I always used as much as possible. As soon as the dog's hand training was completed, I would take each dog for a little run around and adapt every situation that arose to my advantage. In this way, no two training sessions were ever the same, thereby creating the uncertainty and maintaining the dog's interest.

Dead There (Early & General Training)

This is another command that the trainer may use to instruct the dog to retrieve.

Directing the 'Turn' Signal

The correct procedure to follow is to drop him first, then walk up to him quietly, remembering to avoid eye contact at this stage. Upon reaching him, still maintaining silence, grasp his ear and give it a tug whilst at the same time sound off the single short but sharp 'peep' of the turn whistle command, repeating this two or three times. When giving whistle signals remember this, for it is of the utmost importance. All whistle signals must be uttered in short sharp chirps; never fall into the trap of sending long drawn-out signals. Long and lazy signals convey to the dog that, Oh! there goes the whistle, but

Directing the 'turn' signal.

I've plenty of time to respond to it. In other words, long sloppy commands equal long sloppy responses. The command means now, not when the dog might feel inclined to answer to it. So, sharp, brisk commands at all times.

Remember, he learns by association with the example, so be in no doubt, he understands what it is all about and you will see a marked improvement to the 'turn' whistle command immediately after a reprimand such as this. Leaving him on the drop, walk back to where you were when the dog had disobeyed you, face him and signal with your hand pointing in the opposite direction to that which he had been taking, and give the word of command 'Get On' accompanied by the 'turn' whistle signal. You must insist that he turns in the direction that you have indicated. If he still refuses, stop him, walk back quietly and repeat the chastisement. It is tiresome, but nevertheless it is the only way. Remember, you are the top dog in this pack not him.

Discipline (General Training)

A word of warning regarding chastising a dog will not go amiss at this juncture. Before chastising a dog you must never forewarn him of his impending fate by crashing through the undergrowth toward him uttering loud dire threats. Not as unusual a scenario as one might imagine. All that such behaviour will accomplish is to initially frighten the living daylights out of the dog. Furthermore, if it occurs on a regular basis, knowing that dogs have excellent memories, it will not be long, or surprising for that matter, before he will recognise the thunderous approach for what it is, the precursor to a reprimand. From that moment on it will not be long before rapport between the dog and his handler will deteriorate to the extent that control will be lost completely. The dog will become so frightened and distrustful of the trainer that he will run away when he sees or hears the cantankerous approach. Any future prospects of training him will then progressively disappear.

Once you have trained the dog to various whistle, hand and vocal commands, then you may introduce him to hunting for game for real, but not before. Until he is obedient to all commands you must be relentless in striving for consistency. Once the dog has demonstrated over a period of time that he understands what a particular signal means, you will at all times, from then on, insist upon his obedience to it. Some dogs will, through the sheer excitement of the moment, get carried away with the task in hand and dogs, being like children – natural optimists – will occasionally 'try it on'. The trainer must insist at all times, without fail, on the dog's compliance. The trainer who is lackadaisical or inconsistent and thereby fails in teaching the dog the error of his ways, will surely pay the price.

Providing that there is no doubt in the trainer's mind that the dog has deliberately misbehaved, he must deal with each incident equally and with consistency. The dog must always be halted and dropped before being approached. Never indulge in chasing him, for you will probably be on a hiding to nothing, especially if he is in cover, for once he gets into full gear we know he can easily outrun us. At this point let me give another warning. After the dog has stopped running and is on his way back to the trainer he must never be punished. The initiative has been lost and remember he associates everything by example. If he is punished in such a circumstance, the trainer may find that the dog is not so enthusiastic in returning to his trainer in which case retrieving to hand could be damaged.

Advice

An aspect of training that most trainers, amateur and professional alike, do not seem aware of but is of the greatest of importance to understand from the very beginning of training, is that a dog must never be physically punished in the presence of or even within the sight of another. Why? Because they take it personally.

It does not take much imagination therefore, to realise that while training a dog you would be well advised to avoid hunting him during the greater portion of the dog's first season in the field, in the company of your friends who own dogs. There is a very good chance that their dogs are not as well trained as yours and therefore will at some stage misbehave and your friends are not likely to consider your young dog's perspective when venting their wrath upon the offending dog. Another aspect worth considering is that when your friends notice how well you seem to be doing with your dog, envy may encourage a degree of gamesmanship. This is by no means unusual and can manifest itself in a variety of ways, such as gradually encroaching into your young dog's hunting area to break up his ground treatment and confuse him, or 'accidentally' allowing their dog to 'run in' whilst yours is actually retrieving.

Discouraging Game (Intermediate Training)

I have always tried to play safe by avoiding if possible, the problems arising in training in the first place, rather than acting hastily and regretting it. Once your dog is efficient on all whistle and hand signals there will be time enough to start thinking about allowing him to encounter game. If you are aware that there is liable to be game on the ground where you intend to give your young dog a training session, you would be well advised to avoid the potential danger of him stumbling on a rabbit and giving chase. Faced with this situation I would always play safe.

It is important that you park your car out of sight of the training area, for you do not want the younger dog to view what is going on. Leaving the young dog in the car, I would then work the whole area thoroughly with an older well seasoned campaigner to clear the game away. Once I had accomplished this I would return the older dog to the car and putting the younger dog on the lead I would go back to the training area, where I would work the young dog in concentrating on his ground treatment.

You may now relax, confident that apart from perhaps a 'missed' rabbit, there is little chance of a mishap. It is now, when for the first time since his training started, you will get an inkling of the young dog's future potential as regards style, pace and nose when hunting, for if everything has gone to plan with his hand training, probably unnoticed by the trainer for it tends to be an insidious process, the dog will have slowed down, probably quite considerably. Now, for the first time he will be exposed to fresh scent and this should dispel any inhibitions that he has undergone in the hand training sessions. This will 'fire' him up and get him going as never before. Consequently, the handler will be able to assess his 'biddability', his willingness to please or whether he is going to be the type of dog that tends to be headstrong, 'hots up' and wants to do things his way when exposed to the strong scent. If the latter is the case then he will be quite a handful. This is the type of dog with which no risks can be taken and that must be thoroughly trained before he ever gets to see the rabbit.

Disobedience (Advanced Training)

In order to avoid confusion for those of you implementing the Training Plan, and due to the similarities between the 'disobediencies': – Disobeying the 'Return' Whistle; – Drop – Disobedience To; – Discipline; and Disobedience: it is necessary that I place them under separate headings. Once you have trained the dog to the various whistle, hand and vocal commands, then you may introduce him to hunting for game for real, but not before. Until he is obedient to all commands you must be relentless in striving for consistency. Once the dog has demonstrated over a period of time that he understands what a particular signal means, you will at all times, from then on, insist upon his obedience to it. His complete compliance with your commands is essential; the bedrock of training lies in unfailing obedience. Woe betide the trainer who is neglectful in teaching the dog the error of his ways if and when it is required. Providing that there is no doubt in your mind that he is deliberately misbehaving, then you must deal with each misdeed equally and with consistency. You must always drop him first before approaching him, never indulge in chasing him, for we know that once he gets into full stride, he can outrun us effortlessly.

At this point let me give you warning: never chastise a dog once he has turned and is coming towards you, just stand still and welcome him on his arrival. Most important of all, you must never punish a dog whilst he has something in his mouth. In the first place you will most certainly discourage him from retrieving to hand and secondly you could induce 'hard mouth'.

Disobeying the 'Return' Whistle (General Training)

If the dog has been disobedient to the 'return' whistle command, the correction procedure can be quite hard work for the handler, especially if the dog has disobeyed whilst he is in thick cover. The trainer must drop the dog first, then, quietly approach the dog. Nothing will be achieved by ranting and raving at the dog. Upon reaching him, take a firm grip of the scruff of his neck and facing him with the recall whistle clamped between your teeth, take one step back firmly pulling him in toward you whilst simultaneously giving the sharp double 'peep – peep' with the whistle. Whether you like it or not, you will have to repeat this action at least four or five times in quick succession. Every time from then on, without fail, the whole process must be repeated, whenever he disobeys the recall whistle signal. A word of consolation however, provided that you are pedantic enough in correcting the dog's misdemeanours in the fashion outlined, it would be exceptional if the dog's attitude and behaviour as well as his respect for the trainer, did not show a marked improvement over a very short period of time.

Dog Schoolmaster

There are those who advocate the use of an older dog to run with an inexperienced dog acting in the 'schoolmaster' role. I believe that this is just another of the old wives' tales, which abound in the dog-training milieu, and as such are utter nonsense! In the general training sense, all that an old campaigner will do is teach your novice bad habits. The only time that I might use an older dog in the company of a younger dog for training purposes, would be when first introducing a nervous water-shy pup to water. I would, if the pup really looked as though nothing was going to induce him to enter the water, for jealousy's sake, send in a couple of dogs. Under no circumstances would I contemplate running older dogs in the company of inexperienced dogs. A very good maxim for training dogs is 'you, the dog, and solitude'.

Drop – Disobedience (General Training)

Unfortunately, despite taking safety measures regarding clearing the game off a piece of ground, there will be the rabbit or bird that has been 'missed' by the older dog earlier. Needless to say, Murphy's law decrees that this is going to be the one that your younger inexperienced dog is going to 'fall' over. Should he then give chase, as he probably will, there is nothing that you can do in this situation. If you start charging after him, you will only succeed in drawing his attention to the fact that something is wrong and that you cannot catch him. Let us imagine the unlikely event that you do manage to catch him, what are you going to do? If you are confident that the dog is well aware of what he has done because he has been well versed in the 'stop' whistle signal, in which case by running in he has shown it to be a cold-blooded act of defiance, the solution then is simple – punishment on the exact spot where he found the game.

On the other hand, it is folly to punish a young inexperienced dog for a

crime that he is unaware of committing, but, if you do, don't forget that he has an excellent memory. Consequently, not only will you impress on him that something is amiss, he will not forget it. Because as we have seen, dogs learn by association, in correcting him for a crime that he does not understand that he has committed, he will remember the circumstances: scent, then rabbit, plus chase equals punishment. Should you repeat your mistake at a later date, the young dog will also remember that incident very clearly, and you will be one step further down the road to being in grave danger of producing a dog that has been abreacted to scent.
(*see* Neurotic Aversion to Scent, page 100)

Advice

If a young inexperienced dog accidentally finds a rabbit or a bird and gives chase, remember he is only doing what god put him on this earth for. He is a 'hunter' therefore he is only doing what comes naturally. Instead of creating a great big fuss over a futile situation, if you ignore the chase and give him the recall whistle signal once you see him returning, you will then be able to praise him for coming back to you, thereby reducing the little adventure in his mind. By praising him, you have ended the training session on a successful note. Moreover, you have been warned as to the danger of allowing the situation to occur again, and taking into account his excellent memory, you will not return to that particular venue with him, until you are sure that he has forgotten the affair.

Drop – Disobedience To (Intermediate & Advanced Training)

In the case where the dog has deliberately disobeyed the 'drop' or 'stop' whistle signal, you must not let him get away with it, for this command is the lynchpin of all future training. If you do not get one hundred per cent obedience to this crucial whistle command then there can be no expectation of success in the dog's training. Without this, the final deterrent, quite simply, you do not have a trained dog.

Once you have been compelled to implement the following regime you will understand when I tell you that you will not wish to do it too often.

Advice

If the dog has refused the drop whistle, obviously he must still be on the move. Sooner or later he has to stop. You will find that provided he has shown you that he is aware of what the stop whistle command means, even after he has disobeyed it, he will be easy to drop, either by the hand signal or the whistle, or a combination of both, for eventually he will lose his forward motivation.

After succeeding in dropping him, as always you must approach the dog quietly, avoiding eye contact until you can get a grip of him. Take him firmly back to the exact spot where he had disobeyed you. On that spot you will demonstrate your displeasure. Facing him take a firm hold of him at the top of the neck just behind and below his ears, you will then demonstrate who is top dog by glaring up close into his eyes. Believe me, he will not like this, in fact you can almost feel him cringing in your grasp. Give him a good shaking maintaining your stare up close and personal, growling into his face. Finish the chastisement by flapping back his ear and blasting the stop whistle signal short, sharp and piercingly into it. Don't be soft about this treatment. You cannot stress too strongly to him that this is the one signal that must be obeyed. The whole procedure will be clearly understood by the dog, for he

A rabbit skin dummy.

recognises the place where he committed the crime and he also connects the stop whistle command that he defaulted on with your displeasure. For your response to his disobedience is not all that far removed from how his mother would have treated him as a pup when he misbehaved. This type of reprimand will never cow a dog nor break his trust in you. All that is required is consistency.

Dummies

The dummy is quite simply any soft object in varying weights utilised to encourage a dog to retrieve. For the tiny puppy, the retrieving object will simply be a rolled-up sock or a knotted handkerchief, to be thrown in full view of the puppy a few feet in front of him onto a grassy surface. As with all retrieving exercises it cannot be emphasised strongly enough that 'less is most definitely better than more'. You must never overdo the retrieving exercises all the way through training and even to the end of the dog's first shooting season. The inexperienced dog must never under any circumstances get it into his head that every time you chuck the dummy out, that he is going to retrieve it, nor in the future that every shot automatically means retrieve. Throughout his first shooting season, you must only allow him to retrieve perhaps one bird in three. This is to obviate the danger of his acquiring the habit of running into shot.

As in every aspect of gundog training, the handler must be flexible in his or her approach, nothing is cut and dried, what may appear quite acceptable to one dog can be utterly rejected by another. The same applies to dummies, there are dogs who have never picked a canvas dummy in their entire life, Macsiccar Merrit was one. In such cases an acceptable alternative must be found.

As the pup matures, the dummies become more sophisticated. The home-made are feather (mallard wings are excellent) and rabbit or hare fur. These are introduced in the intermediate phase of the dog's education. There are now a vast array of dummies manufactured to a very high standard, which are available from any good shooting merchant.

Dummy Launchers

These are an indispensable tool for both the amateur and professional gundog trainer. They consist of a handle that is hinged in order to insert a .22 blank cartridge into the breech. The launcher is then closed and the specially made dummy is slotted onto the long hollow cylinder which has a small hole at the top. It is from this that when the launcher is discharged the thrust launches the dummy.

Depending how far down the spigot the dummy is slotted will determine the distance achieved by the dummy. I have used the launcher for many years for a variety of training exercises, dropping to shot and water

Dummy launcher.

retrieving. Also, I found them invaluable for simulating a 'line' for the dog, using one of the specially made launcher balls smeared with rabbit scent which are also manufactured by the makers. Launched at a low trajectory, the ball would hit the ground about twenty to thirty metres away, bounce, then roll on for a considerable distance which would provide a 'line' for the dog to follow.

In case of difficulty in your local shops, contact Turner-Richards, Cardigan Street, Birmingham (www.turnerrichards.co.uk).

Chapter Five

E

Ears

The hearing capabilities of a dog are far more intense than ours. In addition to this, they are conscious of a much wider range of sound waves than we are capable of detecting, especially in high frequencies. This is why many dog trainers use the so-called 'silent' whistle. In addition to this the dog's tympanic membrane in the ear is super sensitive to vibration and can sense the impact created by a bird's fall at thirty to forty metres distance. It is in relation to the dog's sense of vibration that many dog handlers reinforce vocal and whistle signals for the dog to 'Hup' with a stamp of their foot. Just as with the power of the dog's sense of smell, it is difficult to quantify his hearing capabilities. For our purposes, suffice to say that we accept that the dog's hearing is a great deal more efficient than ours. This again presents an aspect of training and working a dog that is rarely, if ever, given anything other than the most cursory consideration. It is important to appreciate that there are times when because his ears are so efficient at detecting every sound, lots of which are undetectable to our hearing, he can become confused. In conditions such as a high wind, there is little if any scent and the dog may act peculiarly, to the point that to his handler he appears to be ignoring the vocal and whistle signals. This is commonly called 'whistle deafness'. Gale-force winds appear to generate many more sounds than usually assail the dog's ears and because of the dog's extra sensitive hearing probably create a thunderous buffeting to the extent that the handler's voice or whistle command are distorted in the dog's peripheral hearing or even obliterated completely. Consequently be aware of the fact that in such conditions the dog is probably just confused and therefore it is not a case for berating him.

As I have said, many dog trainers prefer silent whistles. I don't, for the pitch of the whistle sound is controlled by swivelling the barrel of the whistle. Even the slightest thought on this illustrates that the pitch can be altered by the smallest indistinguishable turn of the swivel so that the signal will never be exactly the same, consequently the dog's reaction to it may differ also. I think that perhaps the handler in a field trial will favour this type of whistle, believing that if the judge cannot hear his signals this will go in his favour, I remember Jack Windle, who was quite deaf, telling me that because of the high pitch of these whistles, his hearing aid picked them up and that it could be quite painful. Some time later when it came up in conversation, Tom Laird made the observation that these high tones could actually have a detrimental effect on the shooting, because they could frighten the birds well in advance of the beaters' approach. I don't know, but it is food for thought.

The whistle signal command is the most important and sensitive aspect of dog training. No dog, however efficient his hand training may appear, can be considered as fully trained if the whistle training is incomplete. Even using exact duplicate whistles, no two trainers will emit the same sound even though to our ears the sounds may seem identical.

For example, I had a disagreement with one of my clients and he demanded that his dog be returned to him, one that I had been handling for him in field trials.

A few weeks later I saw him at a trial and discovered on getting the trial schedule that he had entered the dog and was going to handle him. As the trial progressed I could see that he was in the 'line' at the other side and appeared to be doing quite well. Murphy's law then decided that I was called into the nearside of the line. At this point I must say that all my clients' dogs were trained by the same whistles and a set was always given to the client when they came to collect their dog, and they were schooled rigorously in giving the correct whistle signal. No sooner had I uttered a whistle signal than my erstwhile client's dog burst out from heavy cover at the other side of the line and in a matter of seconds was working like clockwork pacing the dog that I was handling. Obviously then, no matter how close to the original whistle command, the dog will remember his trainer and is able to differentiate between his 'new' handler's signals and for an appreciable interval thereafter respond to the original signals that he had been trained to. At the end of the trial my erstwhile client approached me and, apologising for the original difference of opinion, asked me to take his dog back.

(*see* Whistles page 166)

Eye Colour – Hard

Generally speaking a dog with a light yellow, 'hard' staring eye is to be avoided. This colour is not to be confused with the light eye in some of the bird dogs. In the Labrador, curly coat, springers, cockers, there are several shades of eye, from very dark right down the colour scale to light, but the light 'mustardy' unfriendly looking, hard-staring eye is unmistakable. Such an eye, in many instances, denotes an unstable, even mentally disturbed character, which may be so headstrong as to be virtually untrainable. Even the novice should be able to recognise this eye and thereby avoid purchasing the bearer. (*see* Breeder page 12)

Eye Shy

Most dogs to a greater or lesser degree tend to be 'eye shy', that is to say, they do not like eye to eye contact at close quarters. This is probably connected to the fact that in the canine world, eye to eye confrontation represents a hostile challenge. Furthermore there is no doubt in my mind that the human eye is not a pleasant sight to a dog either, possibly due to the fact that we are the only 'animal' that shows the white of the eye. It is therefore most important that when dealing with your dog you bear this in mind, particularly as he comes to hand and especially when retrieving. This does not mean that you look away, of course not! You obviously want to see what is going on, and so the wearing of a flat cap with a peak or a wide-brimmed hat is recommended, thereby shading or shielding the eye from the incoming dog. Instead of staring into his eyes as he approaches, try tilting your head down looking askance at a spot near the top of his legs, so you are not staring into his eyes, yet your peripheral vision is sufficient to see all of the dog's performance. It is feasibly the amateur trainer unwittingly using direct eye contact, that leads to the dog approaching the handler hesitantly, or circling with his head tucked into his chest when in the act of delivering a retrieve.

Unthinkingly, many years ago I changed my glasses for what was then the new type, bifocals with photochromic lenses, which would progressively darken in response to sunlight. I couldn't have envisaged the troubles that were in store for me. From that moment on, even my best dogs would not deliver to hand. It shouldn't have, but this had me completely flummoxed until luckily a few days later I received some photographs that I intended for one of my articles in *Sporting Gun*. The 'mystery' was solved, for staring out at me from the photographs where my eyes should have been were two black discs, no wonder the dogs were reluctant to come into hand.

If at any time when training or even in later years, the dog displays inexplicable behaviour with any aspect of his work, whereas in the past he has performed well, then, stand back and consider that it may not be the dog's fault and there may be a very simple explanation that has not as yet revealed itself to you.

Eye Wipe

This is a situation regarding retrieving that hardly applies in the general mêlée that tends to occur at the formal or rough shooting day where sadly it is all too common to see several uncontrollable dogs running in to shot after a fallen bird and a general tug of war then ensuing between them for the bird.

In the field trial situation 'eye wipe' is much more relevant and important. When game has been shot and Dog A has been sent into the area of the 'fall' to retrieve it and yet after a suitable interval, fails to collect it Dog B is then sent for the game and if he makes good the retrieve, then Dog B could be awarded the 'eye wipe'. However this is completely at the discretion of the judge, for no two retrieves are ever alike and the judge must make his or her decision based on the individual circumstances.

Let us imagine that Dog A was sent for the retrieve but for whatever reason his handler did not manage to put his dog into the area of the fallen bird. Whilst the judge is duty bound after a suitable interval to ask the handler to call his dog back and consequently disqualify the dog from the stake for failure to collect the bird, it may not be considered fair to award an 'eye wipe' to the next dog down, simply because its handler had the good luck to get his dog onto the fall. This is a case for the judge's opinion. Generally speaking though, the dog who successfully delivers the game to hand, is the dog who has gained the 'eye wipe' and extra points are usually earned by the dog concerned.

Advice

A word of warning here will not go wrong. If you are in a field trial and are asked to send your dog for a bird or rabbit that another competitor's dog has failed on, if you have seen the other dog 'mouth' it or if you have a doubt, you are entitled to ask your judge if the other dog had gripped the game. If the answer is yes, then you are within your rights to refuse it without incurring a penalty. You would be wise if on a normal shooting day you observe another dog gripping then refusing to deliver the game, to refrain from sending your dog for the pick-up. The reason being that 'mouthed' or bitten game encourages your dog to also bite the game and thereby 'hard mouth' may ensue. Far better just to walk out and pick up the game yourself.

Eyesight

An aspect which is rarely considered by both amateur and professional trainers, yet its importance is obvious, is the dog's eyesight. What is not so clear to the amateur is that it can explain why the dog behaves in certain ways to particular circumstances. The dog is long-sighted which makes it difficult for him to focus on objects close at hand, consequently the nearer he approaches the area where the target lies, the more he will depend on his scenting powers. This explains why he can see clearly and mark birds down at a great distance. Try watching your dog when shooting ducks at last light, how many times after you were sure that you had missed a bird, he would indicate that you had not. Granted there is a school of thought that says this is because he has heard the shot strike the bird. I am not sure about this, but there is no doubt that the dog can mark these birds in very poor light with great accuracy.

Unlike most humans, the dog is colour blind. He sees only in black, shades of grey or light. It is most important for the trainer to understand and make allowances for this difference when working his dog. If a dog is sent for a bird or a rabbit lying in the furrow of a ploughed field, it is not unusual to see the dog run straight out to his mark only to go right past the game. I have on many occasions seen a dog run right over a bird or rabbit, for the scent may be masked by the direction of the wind and the angle of the furrows. Even if the dog's eyesight registered the shape of the game, it would be a blurred and indistinct image. It is by no means unusual for a dog to be disqualified in a field trial after failing on what to many of the less knowledgeable spectators appeared an easy retrieve.

Similarly, imagine a bird has been shot and has fallen at the lee side of a stream tucked closely into the bottom of a thirty centimetre bank. You have been working the dog on a left-sided cheek wind. It would be understandable for the handler in such a situation to think that this retrieve would be easy. Simply signal the dog to cross over to the right bank, send him up that side of the stream, stop him opposite the dead game, then signal him to cross over to the left, into the wind, almost on top of the bird. It would not be unusual if the dog were to fail on such a retrieve, because the dog does not trust his eyes at close quarters. He relies on his nose, and in this particular scenario the scent from the downed bird will be distorted by the downward swirl of the wind current in relation to the bank of the stream. This fault, if it could be so called, in the dog's close vision manifests itself in many circumstances.

To many novice trainers, poor scent may not be easily recognised. A good yardstick is that any extremes in weather are an indication of poor scenting conditions. It is also important for the trainer to be aware that there are circumstances when scent will vary from very poor to good within a matter of a few metres. A classic example being on a frosty morning where one side of a hollow in the ground or ditch has not been sunlit as yet and a few metres away the sun has melted the frost.

Experts

There are more 'self-elected' experts involved in the dog training field than in any other profession that I can call to mind. Despite the many years that I have been involved in dog training, this enigma continues to baffle me. By the strangest quirk in human nature, it is a fact, that you may ask a man where he got his old banger of a car or you could even criticise his wife and still remain friends, but unless you wish to make a lifelong enemy of him, you must never even hint that his dog has a fault of any kind.

The expert has, by fostering the image, a responsibility to the recipients of his wisdom, even more so if he regularly contributes in the sporting magazines thereby foisting his views upon his readers. Shortly after I had written an article in *Sporting Gun* stating that I had for over twenty years during the summertime used birds which had previously been frozen, I was highly amused to read a report on a field test where the organisers, in an effort to make the test more realistic, used cold retrieves which had previously been frozen. Peter Moxon, in his report, stated that whilst conceding that this new approach held possibilities, he had concerns that the majority of the dogs refused to retrieve half-frozen birds. In my view any semi-skilled trainer, or for that matter enlightened correspondent, would know that a previously frozen bird must be fully thawed before expecting a dog to retrieve it.

I have no particular objection as to whether a man or woman wishes to appear knowledgeable in the ways of the dog or not. Where it becomes irksome to the professional trainer is when the advice from these pundits interferes with the recipient's dog training before the dog is brought to the professional for training. I can only plead with my readers who may be seeking advice, to make certain that the source of their advice has a well-earned reputation, or, better still, dare I suggest it, to stick relentlessly to the advice in my books.

Chapter Six

F

Field Trials

Undoubtedly there will be readers who, upon reading my books will aspire to entering field trials, so it would be remiss of me not to mention the advantages and the pitfalls which all novice field trial contenders, sooner or later, will encounter.

Peter De Lande Longe – a gentleman of the old school.

In my early field trial days I have been known to ask a judge's advice. I have always believed that the only way to learn is to listen to others who have greater experience. I still hold to that view. I have on numerous occasions criticised judging in my magazine articles but, I hasten to add, never on my account but in defence of the readers.

One friend of mine, who, to me, epitomised the best in field trials warrants a mention here, Peter De Lande Longe, a quiet, caring and honest gentleman of the old school, when judging or competing in field trials. Sadly he is no longer with us. Another was Tom Laird, whose Criffel prefix was for over half a century, one of the most recognised in the UK and the USA. I was privileged in that, for many years, Tom was my friend. He was as honest as the day is long, and a superb raconteur with an insatiable curiosity which could have been misconstrued as nosiness, but was merely an interest in his fellow man. Tom also had a devilish sense of humour to which I fell prey on many occasions and he was also one of the best shots that I have ever seen. I have been disqualified from a field trial more than once by Tom, but I never ever resented this, for he was always just.

A pointer drops as grouse flush at a pointer and setter trial.

I am also proud and privileged to have, for twenty-five years, been a close friend of Jack Windle, probably the best psychological trainer that I have ever known, whose 'Jordieland' cockers were renowned worldwide and, I believe, did not go unnoticed within royal circles either. As gundog trainers, I would place Jack and Tom as second to none. The world is the poorer for their passing.

It must be said that it is not within the remit of the writer of a gundog training manual to express any misgivings he has in relation to field trials, for his book is intended merely to instruct the reader in the training of dogs.

Field trials are the only means whereby the public can gain an insight into the quality of the dogs concerned. However, sometimes it is not as cut and dried as all that. If the rules are not that strictly adhered to the results are distorted and thereby the quality of the dog misrepresented. This does damage the breeds, for the prospective breeder or purchaser has no guide to the dog's true standards. The breeders of today are seeking quality and because of showing more interest in the sales potential of the resulting puppies from a mating, they tend to choose the fashionable champion of the moment. However, it may be that the champion in question may not be deserving of the title. I suggest that a more reliable guide to quality is the dog who is consistently in the minor places at field trials. For instance, if you could find a dog that was of the standard of my own bitch, Macsiccar Michele, then I would suggest that such a dog is an animal of quality.

First Season's Experience

If and when all your aspirations regarding your dog's training have been realised, your dog is fully trained. That is to say, he has illustrated that he is steady to shot and to the exciting flush of game, has achieved a good methodical ground treatment with a fair pace, can mark, retrieve and deliver the game to hand gently from land or water, is obedient to hand signals to a blind retrieve and acts appropriately to them at a distance from you, his handler. Then you would be justified in recognising that you have achieved what you had set out to do: you have attained a trained dog, albeit an inexperienced one.

All that is required thereafter is, that the dog receives a thorough schooling in the shooting field in his first season's experience. It is during this time that the trainer will be walking very gently and never taking a risk that may damage the young dog's experience. It is tempting, and indeed occurs far too frequently in training the gundog, that no sooner has the trainer completed the dog's training, than all caution is thrown to the wind in the first few shooting forays. With no further thought to his dog's inexperience the handler tends to ignore him, being more engrossed with his shooting, whereupon all the training is completely undone. It is of vital importance that the shooting man must disregard his love of shooting for the dog's entire first season and become a dog handler first and a shooting man second.

Picking up at your local estate is an excellent way of procuring retrieving practice for the young dog. Beating the game out to the guns is quite another matter. Retrieving game for the guns can also present problems for the dog handler. Whilst it may not be in the interests of the keeper or the guns involved, a wise handler will select the birds that he considers beneficial to his dog's experience. Strong running birds are to be avoided like the plague and considered potentially hazardous for an inexperienced dog. Indeed, it is wise to err on the side of caution by sending a first-season dog for only a few carefully considered runners. (*see* Game page 51)

There are also many hazards in the 'beating' scenario. The handler will immediately recognise when he is in the company of those whose dogs have had only lip service paid to any training. Pattern in hunting tends to be the last thing on the mind of most of those who use their dogs for beating. The beating line through the cover tends generally to resemble utter chaos and therefore is not the place where I would advise the handler to attempt to hunt his inexperienced dog if there is to be any hope in keeping him to a good ground treatment or even keeping him within shot. The only situation that I may consider using a dog in the beating line would be if the dog was a reluctant hunter or just plain 'sticky'. However one day in the line is usually sufficient to cure the problem, whereupon a return to normal training methods would be indicated.

By far the most satisfactory means of giving the novice dog experience in the field is to adhere to the adage, 'you, the dog, and solitude'. Maintaining the ground treatment that you have instilled in the young dog during his first season is of paramount importance. As the dog progressively gains more experience he will speed up to the rate at which he used to cover his ground before his puppy confidence and enthusiasm was curtailed by the training regime. Added to this, as time goes by and his education progresses, he will gradually begin to recognise the various body and foot scents and increasingly associate them with the different species of bird or animal that left them. It is at this stage in the dog's growing experience that the handler must be at his most vigilant and be ever watchful for the signs of his dog's growing eagerness. It is at this time that, due to over-enthusiasm, his pupil may break and pursue the flush.

As his excitement grows gradually and progressively speeds up, another hazard may gradually infringe upon his earlier training regarding ground treatment. Unnoticed by the handler, little by little, the dog will take up more ground in his hunting pattern. It is imperative that as soon as the handler notices this he takes remedial action to curb the fault. The dog is probably unconscious of the fact that he is taking up extra ground for it is a gradual process and is entirely due to the dog's enthusiasm. It could be aptly termed an honest fault, but it is very important that during the dog's first season he must be hunted in a tight pattern and any tendency to take up extra ground be discouraged. Be warned though, punishment should not be uppermost in the handler's mind (*see* Boundaries v Hunting page 5). All that is required is for the handler to work him tightly using his turn whistle when appropriate. The reason for working the dog tightly during his first season is because in his second season he will take up ground naturally and, therefore, if he is allowed too much leeway during his first season, the handler may find that he has difficulty in restraining his charge to hunting within the confines of his imaginary box in the second season. A prime example is the dog hunting out of shot.

During the dog's first season's experience it is vital that all of his training is reinforced and no risks must be taken that may undermine his training. He must be kept steady to the flush, even if by prolonged over-emphasising the drop vocal and/or whistle command, the opportunity of a shot is missed and the game escapes.

Whilst steadiness to game is of utmost importance, so is steadiness to shot and the dog must be seen to drop. There is no point in being lazy about this. If the dog remains standing instead of dropping, remember that is one step closer to him running in, so be pedantic.

Equally as important is the number of retrieves that the dog is allowed

First season's experience.

Dropping to flush.

during his first season. If he is sent for every retrieve he will begin to assume that every shot indicates a retrieve and in no time at all will be running in to shot. Again although it may be tiresome, the handler must not be lazy about this, during his first season the dog must learn that every shot or every retrieve is not for him, so one retrieve in three is indicated.

Some experience in taking a line to a runner is also desirable in the novice dog's first season, but with care. The runner must be assessed by the handler as to its worth. If it is a strong runner, especially a cock bird, unsporting though it may be, put another shot in him. It's better to be safe than sorry. A wounded duck is also to be viewed with suspicion and is likely to be of no value to a young dog, as is a hare. An ideal situation to introduce a young dog to a runner would be a hard-hit hen. Added to this, in sending the young dog after it the handler will be well advised to follow the dog on his first two or three runners.

Retrieving in water at the flight pond or in wet marshes on a cold night can present problems too, especially with a young spaniel, for these dogs feel the cold much more than the retriever breeds. A quick success is essential and ideally a marked retrieve, and this is not as easy as it sounds. Whilst an old campaigner through past experience will 'soldier on' the young dog will quickly become discouraged unless he gets a retrieve to bolster his enthusiasm, whereupon he will appear much keener and largely ignore the cold. It goes without saying that a wet kennel dog should be thoroughly dried before being put away for the night. Many years ago now, I hit upon an idea, albeit accidentally. I had a Datsun ZX 300 at the time and didn't want the dog shaking itself, as they are wont to do, in my nice new car, so I encased him in an old mailbag with a cord through the eyelets around his neck. I used this for years. Imagine how I felt upon discovering that it had been patented and was selling like hotcakes in the pet shops.

A good bag for drying wet dogs.

Chapter Seven

G

Game

As I have said in First Season's Experience (page 46) it is very important when handling a young inexperienced dog, to err on the side of caution in every aspect of his training and never more so than when sending him for running game. If in doubt – don't. There are several good reasons for this. Firstly, when working the novice dog, above all else, you must maintain steadiness to game and in sending an inexperienced dog for running game, you are presenting him with a contradiction to his steadiness training. Consequently, you must ask yourself, if he is steady enough to chance it before sending him for a runner.

Secondly, you should know that there are risks in sending a young, inexperienced dog after wounded game, especially so if the said runner is an old cock bird, a hare, a rabbit or a mallard drake. The first may 'spur' him, the hare or rabbit may kick him and the duck is quite capable of giving him a painful tweak on the nose. If there are other dogs out there searching, then leave it, you do not want your young dog to get mixed up in a 'tug-of-war'. Depending on your dog's temperament, if he tends to be of a sensitive nature, any of these mishaps may put him off retrieving for life, then again, if he is of a bolder stamp, he may decide that he is not going to put up with this sort of treatment and therefore the next time, he will put the ribs in – the very thing you didn't want – 'Hard Mouth'.

Game Sense

This is an aptitude born from the individual dog's accumulated experiences in the shooting field and makes its presence known in a variety of ways. It usually begins to manifest itself during the dog's second or third season. As it is an acquired sense it cannot be taught. I have noticed that in some cases depending on each individual dog's experience, an almost uncanny expertise in game sense coupled with a level of adroitness, far beyond anything taught by me, was displayed by the dog.

For instance we are all aware that many experienced dogs will recognise the sound of the shot striking the bird and upon not being sent for the expected retrieve will give some signal to its owner that the bird had not been missed. Upon being sent, he will return triumphant with the bird. That, to a degree is game sense.

I remember an instance of this occurring at a field trial. Macsiccar Merit had found and flushed a rabbit and dropped instantly. The rabbit was shot and the judge told me to send my dog. Upon my commanding her to retrieve, she did not budge but turned her head and looked at me. I had the strangest feeling, perhaps an instinct that she was trying to tell me something. I turned to the judge and told him that I thought that there was another rabbit there.

He didn't believe me and I don't blame him. To this I remarked, 'Well, if I send her for the dead rabbit and the rabbit gets up from where she's lying at the moment, I take it you will not disqualify me for missing game?'

To this he reluctantly replied, 'OK, then tell her to push it out.' She did, without rising from her position.

The judge was genuinely amazed saying that he'd never seen the like in all his experience. That is game sense. Far fetched though it may seem, there can only be one explanation, that through experience she had learned to put the game up one at a time for the gun. (Perhaps she had come to the conclusion that I was such a bad shot that I couldn't shoot the game if it was flushed in pairs!)

At another trial Macsiccar Michele was hunting in thick brambles out of sight of me at the top of the hill on my right. Suddenly the sound of her activity stopped. I stood still waiting, a shot from the gun down the hill to my left rang out and the gun indicated to the judge that he had a dead rabbit straight out in front of him. I was told to send her. On my command she broke through the cover up on my right, charged down the hill past me and popped her head out of the brambles in front of the man who had shot the rabbit. I noticed that in the still air his gun was still smoking. Normally I would expect my dogs to take a line to ground game, however as the distance between the flush and the sight of the shot rabbit was such a great distance, I had intended to give her a directional signal to get her on to the line. I never got the chance, for she had turned, disappeared and returned with the dead rabbit. That is something that cannot be taught – it is game sense. I have no doubt that there are many of my readers who could relate similar incidents with their dogs.

Through the years I have occasionally seen behaviour displayed by my dogs that far exceeded any training that a dog could possibly be given. I remember being told to retrieve a dead rabbit about thirty metres out to my left. No sooner had my dog set out for the retrieve than a gun fired a shot at another rabbit. Putting aside the heinous crime of shooting over a dog whilst it was retrieving, the rabbit had been wounded and it ran on, over the dead rabbit and disappeared into thick bracken. Obviously the situation for my dog had changed. I was now faced with the task of getting my dog after the wounded rabbit ignoring the dead one. I sent him on, fully expecting him to do the natural thing from a dog's point of view – attempt to pick the dead rabbit. I intended to drop him by whistle beside the dead rabbit and order him to 'Leave It – Get Out'. I didn't need to, for before I had the chance to

Springer winding game in cover.

drop him, he was over the dead rabbit and gone into the rough, shortly after returning with the wounded rabbit.

I have also noticed that when cleaning my guns, if I unconsciously pointed the barrel at an experienced dog, he would seek shelter behind any convenient furniture. That displays to me that a dog realises the killing power of the gun through experience in the field, which could be argued to suggest a close alignment to game sense.

Genetics

Surprising though it may seem, it appears when examining the pedigrees of today that there are many breeders and trainers who just do not have the slightest idea whatsoever about breeding dogs. Only a cursory glance at the modern pedigree illustrates quite conclusively that the breeders' choices throughout the pedigree are an indication that their only guidance in choosing a sire has been their blind subservience in accepting the potential sire's field trial accomplishments.

To the uninitiated, this would appear no more than sound common sense. These are the novices to breeding and gundog training who are the prime target as potential buyers of puppies. The gundog breeder is well aware that this is his market, for the novices are the most likely to be impressed by a pedigree bespattered with red ink.

Whether a dog is a field trial champion or not, is of little genetic worth and most certainly does not necessarily signify quality in the breeding. If the breeder has selected the sire using only field trial accomplishments as his guide, with no regard as to the sire's suitability concerning his ancestors' compatibility with the bitch's predecessors, then the resulting progeny can, at best, be only the result of a random genetic inheritance. As such, even though by luck rather than by good judgement, the resulting litter can be judged a success, any of the descendants from that litter are just as likely to be of a lesser quality. Furthermore, all of the siblings of such random matings are potential carriers of 'slumbering' recessive genes, just waiting to unite with a familial gene in another mating, to spring their nasty surprise in the future.

We ignore the laws of genetics at our peril. For every characteristic which makes its presence known, there is the gene to influence it. Furthermore these genes may be dominant or recessive. The genes responsible for producing the aptitudes that we as breeders would recognise as desirable in the progeny are the result of the uniting of two dominant genes, one from the sire and one from the dam. Through a breeder's random choice of unrelated sires, the quality achieved by one litter is most unlikely ever to repeat that standard in any future progeny, for in the genetical maelstrom that is produced at the time of conception, it is just as likely that two recessive genes could unite, which is termed a double recessive gene, and produce an undesirable trait which hitherto had been dormant for many generations. This may leave the breeder scratching his head and probably blaming the sire for the undesired fault, which of course may not be the case.

Genetic Insight

It is obvious then, that selecting the sire using only his field trial accolades for guidance assuming blindly that this must indicate quality, achieves nothing, for as I have already said, there is no logical pattern to it. The only certain result achieved by such random matings is that the future progeny will be relegated to no more than 'the luck of the draw' and pure chance, and are consequently incapable of maintaining quality in their future descendants. Every dog breeder wishes to breed for excellence. Not only will he or she desire to maintain the good traits in their dogs, they will want to add to these good aptitudes with further favourable traits in the future. This can only be achieved by a systematic breeding plan and carefully selecting the genetically suitable sires. It has to be realised by the breeders that selecting a sire, motivated purely by the sire's field trial accomplishments, is a negative approach. It could be argued that without doubt good progeny can, and do, regularly result from these matings – the problem remains in the sustaining of that quality in the future offspring. In the selection of yet another fashionable sire to mate with the offspring in the future, all that will be achieved is a further fragmentation of the gene pool by the introduction of a new invasion of unrelated genes competing for dominance. The result will be that in the ongoing generations, because there is no systematic breeding policy being used, the progeny will not breed true to type.

To remedy the damage perpetuated by consistently mating out-cross parents and strive for particular genetic aims, the breeder must first select a bitch that is considered to be fault free. Thereafter a sire must be sought that is of equal merit. This is not enough however, for a genetic match must be within the first three generations in both pedigrees.

As a hypothesis, let us imagine that the bitch, while excelling in every other aspect, tended to be a little slower than the breeder would wish. The prime aim then would be to seek out a fast stylish sire who also appears fault free, never overlooking the fact that the two must have that all-important genetical tie-in. If in the fullness of time the litter is born and in the following months one or two of the puppies demonstrate that whilst retaining their mother's favourable talents they also exceed her in style and speed, the breeder could then feel pleased for the mating appears to have been successful. Obviously the dominant genes have united and are manifesting themselves in those two pups.

However, what about the other siblings? Perhaps two or three of these are also showing some similar talents yet not to the same extent. It would not be unusual if a couple of pups did not measure up to the breeder's expectations by manifesting a distinct fault. This phenomenon then indicates that, unbeknown to the sire or the dam's owner, farther back in the litter's ancestry, a dog or bitch had manifested the same fault. Two familial recessive genes have been lurking down through the generations, one in each of the immediate ancestry and have combined to form a double recessive gene and thereby gain power. The fact that the other pups from the litter never show any sign of this fault throughout their working lives means nothing, for they also are potential carriers of that same recessive gene, which is lying dormant ready to manifest itself in the future.

If the litter is such an unforeseen but unfortunate outcome, for the future mating of his favourite bitch, the breeder would pursue his desire to enhance the speed of her progeny by seeking out another sire. For this mating he would adopt a different approach by using an out-cross sire, yet one who shows no apparent faults and is a fast and stylish hunter. To qualify as an out-cross, this dog must show no related ancestry in the first three generations. By employing the use of the out-cross, the breeder is obviously attempting to fragment the fault previously shown in her past litter. If all is well in the future and the pups are proven to be a success, the breeder could then attempt with these progeny to mate back into a familial ancestral tree.

On the other hand, the resulting litter may not be exhibiting any serious genetic faults, yet have not lived up to the breeder's expectations in relation to speed. If one or two are bred from, the shining properties that had not manifested themselves in their own siblings could very well be realised in this next generation.

Whilst the status of Field Trial Champion need not necessarily indicate quality, the field trial results may still offer the breeder a reliable insight in his search for a top-class animal. It can be assumed that those dogs that figure consistently in the awards, although not necessarily winners, could safely be regarded as quality animals, for not unusually, it may be simply a case in which the dogs were alright but the owner's face just didn't fit. It can be seen then that the prospective breeder need not confine his choice of a sire to the Field Champions of the moment. In contemplating a dog who has been regularly placed in these events yet never been the winner, there is every reason to believe that he could be the true 'champion'.

Also there are many honest breeder-trainers who will be only too pleased to share their expertise and help the novice with his questions.

At this stage it is important that, if for no reason other than it is interesting, you ought to know a little about the pedigree.

The first three generations, that is sire + dam, grand sires + grand dams and the great grand sires + great grand dams, exert the most dominant influence upon their progeny's potential capabilities through genetical inheritance. On conception the chromosomes from each parent divide equally, 50% of the genetic legacy from each parent is donated to the progeny, consequently the donation from each grandparent is 25% and it follows that the eight great grandparents' legacy is 12.5% each. These percentages however are not cut and dried, for related ancestors further back in the pedigree can significantly alter them. It is also possible for the predominant influences to be further significantly affected by line breeding.

The desirable attributes from dogs' ancestors further back than the first three generations in the pedigree can, by skilful line breeding, be strengthened greatly to the extent that, from being in a minor position of influence they can exert a much more important influence upon the progeny.

Looking at the pedigree on page 74 you will note that, between the box containing the sire's name and the lower box containing the dam's name, there is a main central horizontal line running through the pedigree. All dogs and bitches in the upper section of the pedigree are said to be on the sire or paternal line. These dogs and bitches named in the sire's half of the pedigree are considered to exert a less dominant influence in their genetic legacy than the inheritance from the dam's maternal line, the dogs and bitches which are named below the medial line on the pedigree.

Clearly then, it can be seen that not only do the first three generations of the pedigree, by and large, exert the most influential role in the chromosomal inheritance received by the progeny, but that this is further divided between the effects generated by the sire and the dam lines and that the dam's line is the most influential.

I am not on my own in this opinion, for the dam's dominant role has been recognised down through the years by many authorities. It has merely been clouded in the post-war years by some stud owners dismissing it as a counsel of perfection.

It follows then that the sire can only, at best, endorse the quality of the progeny. It is therefore nonsense to speak of dominant sires who will 'stamp their likeness upon the breed'. Generally speaking therefore, in viewing a pedigree, the potential gundog breeder should devote his greatest consideration to the maternal line, for it is within this line that you would wish the preponderance of quality dogs and bitches to appear. This is not to imply that no consideration should be apportioned to the sire line. It is merely suggesting that it should not be granted an exaggerated role, overriding the importance of the dam's influence. In accepting that the sire's role is one of maintaining the quality of the offspring, then careful examination of his background is demanded also. Therefore, if there are two or three dogs, or preferably bitches in his immediate ancestry, who appear to be related to dogs or bitches in the dam's ancestry, careful consideration of those particular ancestors' capabilities would be desired. By doing so, the breeder would be forming a sound breeding policy for the future, which is a vast improvement on a purely hit or miss breeding policy.

(*see* Line Breeding page 90; Macsiccar Michele Kennel Club records page 63; Lineage page 93; In-Breeding page 74; Inheritance page 77; Out-Cross Breeding page 105)

Get In (Early & General Training)

This is a very useful command and the gundog puppy should be made familiar with it from a very early age. At or around three to four months old, whilst you are taking him for his daily scamper, find an area of rough grass, sparse reeds or thinly distributed bracken, attract his attention, lean down and point into the 'cover' and tell him to 'Get In'. Your early attempts at this may or may not be successful, for there is a significant deal of evidence to suggest that even pups from the same litter display a great deal of variance in their enthusiasm to enter cover. It has to be said that a hunting dog that will not face cover isn't worth a jot. So what at first may appear a rather insignificant little exercise is in fact a very important one, for you are preparing the way for his future when real training will begin. It is because of this need to encourage his interest in cover as soon as possible that causes me to relent in regard to giving tit-bits. If the pup shows a marked reluctance to enter the rough patch, attract his attention and let him see you throwing the morsel a short way into the cover. It is also important not to entice him into brambles, nettles or heavy gorse cover at an early age. Just like us, the dog does not like to be pricked, even considering the obvious verve that older dogs display in entering the roughest of cover. This is purely due to the older dog's excitement at encountering scent and past experience having taught him that such places hold game.

Get On (Early & General Training)

This is the command you will always use at the point when, as a puppy he is merely being allowed a scamper about during exercise and has stopped momentarily, perhaps to investigate some interesting scent. If this order is given from the puppy's earliest days, he will respond to it, as he does with the 'Hup' command and accompanying hand signal. By the time training starts properly, he will be so familiar with it that he will react to it automatically. When training begins properly, this is the command given to start him hunting from the 'Hup!' position.

Get Out / Go Back (General Training)

These are the commands used during training to send the dog back to an unseen dummy, initially along the side of a wall and in later training it is utilised in the 'three dummy' exercise. The aim being to accustom the dog to associate the command in the shooting situation with 'getting out' to a blind retrieve.

Gone Away (Early & General Training)

Again this is an order used from the very beginning in preparation for when the serious training begins. By using this verbal command at the very beginning of the pup's introduction to the big world outside his kennel, as with the 'Get On' signal, the pup will obey it without question. As you walk with the pup in his early exercises, you will notice that every now and again his nose will detect an interesting smell. As soon as you see this, simply tell him 'Gone Away', gesticulating with a wave of the hand and walk on. He will soon get the meaning. This is the command you will use in his future shooting career whenever he appears to be pottering around recently vacated 'seats' or areas of strong scent that have been recently vacated. There can be nothing more irritating than a pottering dog.

Gun Nervous

This is quite common and can be caused in a variety of ways, usually mismanagement or thoughtlessness in the part of the owners. (I never cease to wonder at the stupidity of owners who are regularly seen at game fairs and clay busting clubs trailing a little puppy along.) The tympanic membrane in the immature puppy is not fully formed until around seven months old and is very sensitive to sudden noises. It is not at all unusual for the new owner of a gundog puppy to let curiosity get the better of him and fire a shot from a shotgun to see if this diminutive little pup is 'gun-shy'. Gun nervousness can be caused accidentally as well. I have known of several dogs who were the victim of Guy Fawkes night, even one that fell victim to a sudden unexpected loud peal of thunder. A very common cause of being gun nervous is quite simply thoughtlessness by the owner in discharging the gun whilst the dog is sitting in front of him, so that the dog receives the full blast of the report. There is no real cause for alarm, though undoubtedly it indicates that if any success in training the dog to work in the field is envisaged, a certain amount of extra work will be required to alleviate it, but nothing that is beyond the capabilities of the average dog owner.

Occasionally, I would be asked an intriguing question by shooting companions concerning their latest gundog acquisition. Briefly it would run along the lines that having trained their dog 'successfully', on the first day of the dog's introduction to shooting for real, he would be hunting well and then for some strange reason suddenly refuse to hunt and would not stray from his handler's heel. As this situation is precisely why I have created the 'training plan', hopefully it will no longer occur.

It is a classic case of the training being rushed through by the handler. The young dog is telling his master that he does not like the gunfire: it's as simple as that. The handler has, upon noting that the pup did not appear to be unduly worried regarding the blank pistol, assumed that everything was alright and carried on through the training prematurely. It is a case of late gun nervousness.

Advice

The cure for the gun nervous dog suggests itself, for it is merely common sense. If the report of the gun is obviously unpleasant to the dog, he must be taught to associate it with something pleasant. From the very moment that the owner first realises that something is amiss, he must enlist the help of an assistant.

If the dog is kept in a kennel, then the solution to the problem will be that much simpler. Arrange with the assistant to enter the dog's kennel run and to stand over the dog with his dinner. As soon as the assistant hears the report from the blank firing starter pistol, he or she must immediately put his dinner down in front of the dog. Initially you must fire one shot only, never more than one shot, at a distance of around twenty metres. The assistant will then report to you the dog's reaction. At this distance I would be surprised if the dog showed any reaction at all. However, if the dog has shown a reaction, you must increase the distance from where you fire the shot by approximately four metres, until such times when the assistant reports that all is well, then each day decrease the distance from where you fire the pistol by about two metres. The dog must not be fed at any time before this exercise. With the house dog it is slightly different, for it is very difficult to ensure that the family do not take pity on him and give him tit-bits. In the case of the house dog, obviously there is no kennel, so you must find an area of ground suitable for carrying out the daily routine. The park is out, however if you are training the dog it must be assumed that you have a training area somewhere. You must then, if it is a fair distance away enlist the help of an assistant and travel to the area. From then on the procedure is exactly the same. I reiterate that at no time must you be tempted to fire more than one shot. Furthermore, you must make sure that the shot is never fired near buildings, thick woods or in a steep-sided valley. This is to avoid the production of an echo.

It must also be noted that the sharp crack of the starter pistol is notably different to the duller flatter note from a dummy launcher, which in turn has a different sound to that of a 410 – twenty – or twelve-bore shotgun. Therefore, it is essential that a gun nervous dog must go through the full gamut of gunshot before the cure can be considered a success.

This is one of those exceptional circumstances when I would deviate from my principles, for the gundog trainer must always be prepared to adapt his methods to suit the situation. I would therefore advocate that the handler fill his pockets with 'goodies' for the dog's rewards during this time and even on his first few shooting forays.

If the dog is merely gun nervous, this regime should cure the problem.

Gun Shy

Fortunately this is not at all as common as the average gundog owners may think. In most cases it is simply gun nervousness, which as we have seen, is curable. Gun-shyness is a genetically inherited trait and as such, unfortunately, there is no remedy.

Chapter Eight

H

Habits

If you have purchased a part-trained pup, you may be lucky inasmuch as he will not display any serious bad habits. However, there may be bad habits already ingrained that will present problems in his future training. The format in which the dog is trained should be implemented in such a way as to prevent bad habits forming in the first place, encouraging good habits to be formed instead and by no means least important, in such a fashion as to prevent the young dog from realising that he is being trained. This is not at all difficult to achieve. It is simply a matter of the trainer not allowing a set regime to develop by varying the format each day. This becomes progressively easier as the dog's training develops. The trainer must always be ahead of the game. In other words, the handler must teach him or herself to be aware and envisage the risky possibilities pertaining to every situation and training exercise, then take steps to avoid them before the young dog is exposed to them. Prevention is always better than cure.

Hand Signals

These must always be made clearly and distinctly, especially when directing the dog at distance. Furthermore these must not be overdone, nor so frequent that the dog becomes confused.

(*see* Association – Learning By page 2; Behavioural Boundaries page 5)

Hand Training (General Training)

This encompasses the embryonic stages for all training, from verbal commands, hand and whistle signals, sitting and staying at distance, and early retrieving exercises. As with all foundations these are of the most importance if success in training is to be realised.

All training should be carried out on ground that is devoid of game, people and other dogs. Remember, 'you, the dog, and solitude', so the local park is out. At or around six months old or more, is an appropriate time to begin hand training. By this time, if you have carried out the little 'exercises' during the dog's formative months you should by now have a very good idea

All eyes on their trainer.

regarding his temperament. In these initial hand training sessions there is no harm in chucking the occasional dummy for him to retrieve, but always at the beginning of the training session, never at the end. A little thought on this should make the reasons obvious. At the beginning of the lesson, the dog will be fresh and keen, towards the end he will not be so lively and eager, and therefore the chances of success are not so assured. Again with keenness in mind, ration these retrieves to perhaps one every other session.

In his early months you will have given him certain commands and little exercises, as a result of which gradually, without his realising it, his knowledge is increasing and it should continue to do so throughout his training and future experience.

In the early stages of hand training, the lessons should be kept as simple as possible. Remember, the object in all training is to dwell on success, avoiding the failures as much as possible. Initially these little exercises should be short in duration, ten to fifteen minutes per day is far more likely to cultivate success than two hours at the week end.

I have gone on record many times in saying that there is no such thing as a 'bad' dog. As with us humans, the maladjusted can be a product of their environment as children, and the same can be said for dogs. To put it simply, you would not leave a dog chained up for life and expect him to have a kindly nature.

There is no such thing as a bad dog. There are bad owners, but deceit just does not exist in the dog's nature. Therefore, if you have not succeeded in some particular aspect of his training, it is most probably your fault, not the dog's, for somewhere down through his 'learning chain', you have failed

Macsiccar Michele's Certified Kennel Club Field Trial Records as of 5th February 1981

7/8-11-75	Scottish Gundog Assoc	Certificate of Merit	Novice Stake
17-11-75	Scottish Spaniel Club	Certificate of Merit	Novice Stake
12/13-11-76	North of Scotland Gundog Assoc	Second	Novice Stake
15/16-11-76	Scottish Spaniel Club	First	Novice Stake
18/19-11-76	Gamekeepers National Assoc	Second	Novice Stake
22-10-77	Antrim & Down Springer Spaniel Club	Cerificate of Merit	Open Stake
3-11-77	Lothian & Borders Gundog Assoc	Reserve	Open Stake
31-10-77 & 5-11-77	Scottish Gundog Assoc	Second	All Age Stake
9/10-11-77	Scottish Spaniel Club	Certificate of Merit	All Age Stake
10-12-77	South West Scotland Gundog Assoc	First	Open Stake
14-01-78	**Irish Spaniel Championship – Dunmurry, Co Kildare**		**Diploma of Honour**
4/5-10-78	English Springer Spaniel Club of Scotland	Reserve	All Age Stake
2-11-78	Lothian & Borders Gundog Assoc	Certificate of Merit	Open Stake
7/8-11-78	Strathmore Working Gundog Club	Certificate of Merit	All Age Stake
7-12-78	Scottish Field Trial Assoc	Certificate of Merit	All Age Stake
1/2-10-79	Gamekeepers National Assoc	First	Open Stake
3/4-10-79	English Springer Spaniel Club of Scotland	Certificate of Merit	All Age Stake
5/6-10-79	Lothian & Borders Gundog Assoc	Reserve	Open Stake
13-10-79	Highland Gundog Club	Third	Open Stake
5-11-79	Strathmore Working Gundog Club	Reserve	All Age Stake
30-11-79 & 1-02-79	Scottish Field Trial Assoc	Third	All Age Stake
5/6-12-79	English Springer Spaniel Club	Reserve	Open Stake
8-12-79	South West Scotland Gundog Assoc	Certificate of Merit	Open Stake
30-01-80	Forth & Clyde Working Gundog Assoc	Certificate of Merit	Open Stake
3/4-10-80	Gamekeepers National Assoc	Certificate of Merit	Open Stake
4/5/6-12-80	Scottish Field Trial Assoc	Reserve	All Age Stake
20-12-80	South West Scotland Gundog Assoc	Certificate of Merit	Open Stake

him. So keep that in mind whilst correcting him – it will make you a better trainer.

As I have said, by this time you should have your pupil's personality well 'sussed out'. If your dog is rather an outgoing rumbustious character, then you could have a job on your hands. This is the type of dog that will test your mettle as a trainer by constantly 'trying it on' and testing out his 'behavioural boundaries'. Sussing you out, so to speak! By the same token, the more sensitive dog could be classed as a veritable godsend to the novice trainer, for he will rarely disobey you. In addition to this in my view and undoubtedly a matter for controversy, the more timorous of the dogs would appear to me, in the main, to be of a more superior intelligence than their more boisterous counterparts.

The following may come as a shock to people who knew her, but probably the most sensitive dog I have ever trained was 'Macsiccar Michele'. I bought her from Stan Lewis for seventy-five pounds. Upon seeing her at a trial a year

Increase your backward steps by two each day until you can leave him on the 'drop' and walk back twenty paces.

later, he offered me one thousand pounds for her. She was by Esther Thomson's F.T. Champion, Rivington Santa Claus (a particularly sensitive dog) out of Stan Lewis's Lewstan Busy.

Michele was also the most intelligent dog that I ever owned. Her field trial records speak for themselves (see page 63). She was never out of the awards in twenty-six field trials. I wouldn't like to count the number of field trial winners and champions in her descendants.

I have said in Breeding, (page 13) that one fault is one fault too many! I stand by that. It cannot be contested either that sensitivity is a fault and therefore not to be bred from. Perhaps then, with some validity, I could be accused of flying in the teeth of my own convictions. Be that as it may, I prided myself that I knew enough about genetics to be able to negate the sensitivity by judicious matings. My reasoning was to counteract her genetically inherited temerity by mating her to strong first class sires, such as George Drummond's F.T.W. Drumbro Dally by Tom Laird's F.T.W. Criffel Jet, out of F.T.Ch. Drumbro Daisy. Another strong sire I used was a non-competing trial dog, that I sold to Dr John Powell, whilst I retained the breeding rights: Blackmountain Don by F.T.Ch. Rytex Rex out of F.T.Ch. Criffel Cherry, a full brother to my own F.T.W. Macsiccar Merrit. I also used my own F.T.W. Macsiccar Commanche by F.T.Ch. Don of Bronton, out of F.T.W. Macsiccar Mavourneen, another very bold bitch. My hunches were obviously correct for I could not begin to count the number of top-class trial dogs that have resulted from these matings.

In an effort to get at the genetic inheritance of my erstwhile favourite bitch F.T.W. Macsiccar Auchtertyre Donna, I mated her to Robson of Gwibernant, who was by Gwibernant Ashley Robb out of Macsiccar Auchtertyre Donna, and although this mating produced Macsiccar Mint, the Kennel Club Spaniel Championship 1980, in my opinion, it was the poorest litter that she ever produced.

Hand Training – Sitting at Distance (General Training)

Always be mindful that at the beginning of each new lesson you must exercise patience with your pupil, for this is something entirely new to him. Initially he does not know what you require from him. No two dogs are alike and there are those who are quicker on the uptake than others.

The most important hand training lesson of all is to teach him to sit and stay at distance. After a few minutes when the dog has been allowed a little scamper about to run off 'steam', call him up to you and make a fuss of him, step back and raise your hand palm outwards towards him in what by now must be a familiar signal to him and command 'Hup'. As soon as he has complied, step back, raise your hand again and repeat the 'Hup' command. Keep stepping back for approximately three metres.

Now it would not be surprising if he started to get up and follow you, or to belly crawl (cockers are great belly crawlers). This is because he is not sure about this new lesson and simply wants to stay with you. It is very important that your demeanour does not alarm him at this sensitive stage of his training, so do not alarm him by rushing back to him. Just walk back and quietly take him by the scruff of the neck and return him to the exact spot and commence the whole rigmarole all over again. Do not persist with this for too long. If after a couple of abortive attempts he appears not to be co-operating, forget it for that day, remember he has an excellent memory and there is always tomorrow.

When you have succeeded in his staying at three metres, walk back to him, make a great fuss of him, then let him have a scamper before returning to the kennels. In the days to come, just increase the distance slightly each day and you will find that he will soon get the message.

This lesson must be learned to perfection by the dog, for it is the cornerstone on which all future training is built. Until you can sit a pup down and leave him at a distance with confidence, there is no point in continuing with any further training.

Every day the lesson should follow the same format, that is, a little scamper, followed by, every other day, a small retrieve, 'Hup', walk backwards, pause, then return and praise him.

A small but rather important point at this stage. Never walk the dog back to his kennel on the lead if he is to be immediately interred. Upon arrival at his kennel, let him have a little run around, call him up to you, praise him and then put him into his kennel. This procedure is to prevent him from regarding the lead as the precursor to being locked up. It is equally important to remember that you must never lock the dog up after a failure to brood on his own. Always complete the day's tuition on a successful note by giving him a simple task thereby enabling you and the dog to end the lesson on a happy note.

Hand Training – Returning to Whistle (Early & General Training)

Once you have achieved success with the sitting at distance lesson, you may introduce a little progression, a small step forwards in the training regime. Occasionally, call the dog up to you from sitting at distance, with the small pea-less whistle by giving the return signal of two rapid little sharp repetitive 'peep-peeps'. In conjunction with the whistle signal, crouch down and make a patting motion with your hand. (*see* figure page 95)

You must be careful how you go about this. Every time he is on the drop, pause for a minute or two, let him see your hand putting the whistle in your mouth, keep it there, then two out of every three times walk back to him with the whistle still in your mouth and praise him for remaining on the drop. This is admittedly a small point, but it is nevertheless of great importance. It is, as with all training important to keep him guessing. Never allow a dog to anticipate what is coming next.

Hard Mouth

It may interest the reader to know that the first gundog I purchased had jaws on him like a veritable gin-trap. I must have been pretty wet behind the ears, for it did not register with me that anything was amiss, despite noticing that the 'trainer' had great difficulty using both hands to wrench the dummy from Skip's grasp. Well, we've all got to start learning somewhere.

Thankfully, there are not the amount of genetically inherited hard-mouthed dogs that circumstances might suggest. Indeed, I must confess that I have never seen one. In making such an admission, I fear that someone out there is about to shoot me down in flames. However, there are unfortunately, all too many dogs who are hard mouthed through bad handling, not to mention the kids endlessly chucking something for the dogs to retrieve then roughly pulling it from their jaws. Sheer thoughtlessness by the trainer can easily introduce a hard mouth when common sense could have avoided it. Ask yourself, what are you asking the dog to do when sending the dog to retrieve something? You expect him to pick up the retrieve and bring it back to you. Consider this then, if you were asked to pick up an empty plastic bucket, you could achieve this with the minimum pressure of your fingers. Then again if the same bucket was filled with water, you would have to grip it tighter. It should be obvious that in a puppy's early retrieving lessons the

Sufficient experience in retrieving dummies is of paramount importance.

dummy should be as light as possible in weight, thereby not encouraging him to grip.

It is also of the utmost importance that a young dog is not introduced to fur or feather game prematurely. He must go through the whole gamut of retriever training in proper sequence.

Various lessons are to be learned in safeguarding against 'hard mouth' developing in the young dog. Initially, the dummies have to be light in weight and as the dog gets older the weight may be gradually increased. It is also a good idea that when the young dog comes into hand, the trainer does not remove the dummy straight away but leaves it in the dog's mouth for a few seconds whilst praising and stroking him, and tickling him under the chin is not a bad idea either, before gently removing his prized possession. The idea is to get the dog to associate coming into hand as a pleasurable experience. If in the early retrieving exercises the handler tends to snatch at and remove the dummy too soon, this can encourage the dog to come in head down and, or, circle around the trainer. Worse still, it may make him clench his teeth and take a firmer grip. Staring into the approaching dog's eyes will also encourage the dog to come in with head down and attempt to circle the handler. Leave the dummy in his mouth for a short time before removing it.

Care of his mouth on delivery is also paramount. You must never pull a dummy out of the dog's mouth. Press it up and back gently in the dog's mouth then he should release it. Another approach is to firmly grasp the dog over the top of his muzzle and squeeze his top gums. There are some trainers who advocate putting their foot over the dog's front paw and exerting pressure on it in order to give pain, releasing the pressure the moment that the dog relinquishes the dummy.

Leave express instructions while you are at work that the children are not to be allowed to throw things for the dog or to snatch anything from his mouth. Even after all training has been completed, it by no means suggests that the dog is 'out of the woods' pertaining to the danger of developing hard mouth. Probably one of the worst scenarios which would appear at times to be specifically designed to encourage hard mouth in the dog, is at the formal shoot. This is where you are picking up, probably trying to give your young dog some experience. Even although the 'guns' are well aware that there will be a plethora of 'pickers up', there is always one who, despite seeing your dog down after a bird, will nevertheless send his dog also, which is usually fatter and much older than your young dog, whereupon the bird is wrenched from the young dog's grasp. This is usually due to the 'gun's' enthusiasm and is not meant in a malevolent way.

In regarding hard mouth, it would be a most unusual dog that has never bitten a bird. If you see a dog bringing back a runner with clumps of vegetation between his jaws and the bird with its head down, the tale is told. Probably getting tired after a long chase the bird has tucked into the vegetation. Upon its discovery by the dog it has struggled, necessitating the dog to get a grip of him. The uninitiated might with some degree of justice comment 'hard mouth'. This, of course, is not necessarily so as there were extenuating circumstances. It is for this precise reason that in field trials the judge is meant to look for 'the best dog on the day', ignoring what might have occurred on another day.

There is no cure for 'hard mouth'. If you are in the training game for any length of time, you might hear about nonsensical remedies such as wrap the skin of a hedgehog around the dummy, such old wives' tales are no more than amusing.

Heel (General Training)

This is not, by the widest stretch of the imagination, a difficult task yet especially with the hunting breeds, can develop into a silent war of attrition. The success or failure of this particular aspect of training depends greatly on two things: firstly the age when the dog is first introduced to heel keeping, and

Labrador at heel.

secondly, the trainer's determination to implement zero tolerance. The older the dog the more difficult the task will be, for not only is he getting more mature but he is becoming more set in his ways and forming his own ideas, and may not take kindly to any restraint. He will also be building body weight and increasing his strength, which will aid him in resisting the pull of the lead. A semi-mature Labrador with a constant pull will quickly make the trainer's fingers numb and will tire his arm quite quickly. The trainer's determination and consistency in tirelessly getting the message through to him is paramount. Remember dogs are perpetual optimists. If you relent once, they will always have a go. You must be firm and strong. Little mild pulls on the lead gradually increasing in strength are no use whatsoever. You must get the message through to him by vigorously yanking him back into heel the instant he pulls out.

(*see* Case Hardening page 16)

The leather collar set-up is, in my opinion, as good as useless for this exercise. Remove it and replace it with the rope choker lead. It must be recorded here at this point, that in built-up areas a dog running free without a collar is illegal and is classed as a stray. You must be sure that if perchance he should break free – and it can happen – you are confident that he will not run away. Again with a view to being one step ahead of the game, you should

Rope choke lead.

Labrador walking to heel.

initiate these lessons in an area far away from urban conurbations. Always play safe.

Straight away I must warn you that it is the hunter breeds that will test your mettle. There are those trainers who will initiate heel obedience from a very early age. Whilst by doing this they undoubtedly make life a lot easier for themselves, I have never adhered to this policy when teaching a hunter to walk to heel. It was always my preference with the hunting breeds to get them out there hunting before I initiated heel restraint. Unarguably this made my task that much more difficult, inasmuch as the dog had been stimulated in hunting and therefore had become conditioned to the freedom of it. I must confess though, I never strove for any real strict heel-keeping for a hunter, being satisfied if he did not pull on the lead. That is of course only my opinion, but is formed from the real possibility that a dog's later hunting prowess can be subdued if the heel keeping regime is too severe. I was always much more diligent with heel keeping pertaining to a no-slip dog.

A group of Labradors and a springer all walking to heel.

Hi–Lost (Intermediate Training)

It is a moot point as to the usefulness of this much overdone command. It is used mainly to indicate to the dog that there is something out there to find that he has not marked. Very often this command is used in conjunction with the command given when the dog has been told to 'Fetch It', or 'Dead There'. There is no point in giving this command until such times as the dog's education has reached the stage when you think he is ready to be introduced to the 'blind' or 'unseen' retrieve.

As I have said this is a much over-used command by handlers and on the shoot a noisy handler is an extreme pest to all around him. Some handlers seem to repeat it continuously until the dog finds what he has been sent for. This is obviously done in the mistaken idea that it will encourage the dog. It will not! All that will be achieved is that the dog's concentration will be broken, he will become confused and probably disheartened by the continuous verbal barrage, eventually abandoning the search.

Hiss

It is a useful tip in handling the working dog to send him a warning when it looks as though he is indicating that he is about to play you up. The verbal 'His-s-s-s-s!' is invaluable for this. The hissing sound used in this context as a warning, is easily accomplished. Remember the dog learns by association. At all times, from puppyhood for the rest of the dog's career, whenever you have need to scold him, simply administer the chastisement, then immediately accompany it with hissing at him. Thereafter he will quickly register its meaning even whilst he is busy hunting. This is an extremely important little trick whilst hunting a dog in a field trial, for we know that one cannot chide a dog in these affairs.

As to whether the dog hears it, there is no question – remember his superior hearing powers. A similar ruse employed by experienced handlers is, whenever the dog is chastised the trainer will accompany the punishment by producing and flourishing a large handkerchief. The end result is the same, in that if, when hunting in a field trial, the dog sees the large handkerchief being flourished, he will tread warily.

Chapter Nine

I

In-Breeding

Deciding to breed with two closely related animals is a course of action not to be taken lightly. To most breeders these days the very term 'in-breeding'

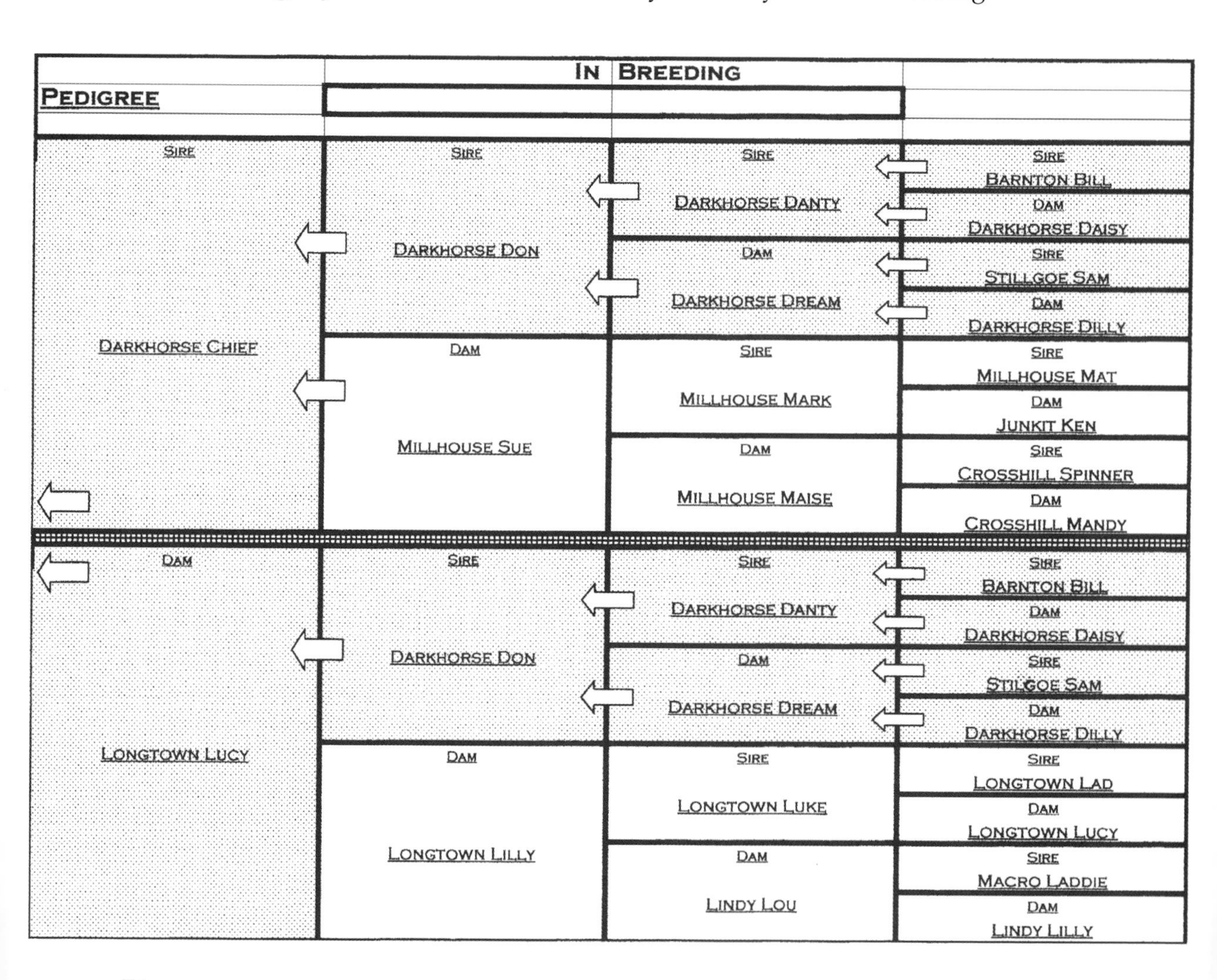

seems to strike terror in their hearts, so it would seem an unnecessary caution. Under no circumstances once undertaken, should in-breeding be repeated within the next two successive generations of the progeny.

Apart from the not unusual accidents that may occur in the busy kennel environment resulting in the mis-matings between a son and his mother, a daughter with her father, a brother to sister, in-breeding is rarely intentionally indulged in. When it is, it will be implemented by the knowledgeable breeder and with caution, hopefully to gather together some semblance of genetic unity in the offspring's inheritance. Such a mating would be warranted if due to past breeders' mating policies, the pedigree illustrated that the first three generations were all unrelated or at best only distantly related. Breeding with unrelated, but fashionable, sires to the bitch is a negative approach, for if even by chance a good litter is brought about, the probability of any continuance in quality in the future offspring can be at best termed remote. The results of a successful in-bred mating can be spectacular. Even so, the breeder must not be tempted to repeat it with another close-bred dog with the progeny, for it would most likely result in disaster.

The nearest in-bred mating that I would consider advisable would be to breed a half-brother to a half-sister, granddaughter to a grandfather, uncle on the sire's line to an aunt on the dam's side, or less courageously two full cousins. (I feel sure that there are those who will disagree.) In figure Line Breeding (page 91) in the third generation of the maternal line, the stronger evolutionary influential line, 'Drumbeat Duster' is the full litter brother to 'Drumbeat Maisie'. In breeding with their immediate offspring, 'Drumbeat Dare' and 'Drumbeat Dulcie', who are half-brother and half-sister to one another with one of the resulting progeny being 'Drumbeat Dora', the breeder has brought about an in-bred mating.

It must be understood that by no stretch of the imagination can any kind of breeding, no matter how well programmed, be looked upon as magical, for nothing must be taken for granted. Nothing is ever certain in the mating game. Obviously the motivation for an in-bred union is to hopefully co-ordinate certain good aptitudes noted in the parents and pass them on to the progeny. The danger is always present, however, that whilst the aim is to target the familial genes for advantageous traits, the recessive gene may also find a familial link and thereby gain equal dominance resulting in unwanted traits appearing in the progeny. By in-breeding, we can be sure of only one thing, which is that the progeny will display an excess of their genetical inheritance. Either the progeny will be very good and the breeders may congratulate themselves, or the progeny may display an excess of genetic faults. What the breeder could reasonably expect would be a fair distribution of good and bad genetical results.

Any hope of success can only come from a planned consistent pattern. The breeder of dogs does not take the decision to implement an in-bred mating lightly. Indeed, the only incidence when such a mating may be contemplated as worthwhile would be if the dam's pedigree indicated that there were no related dogs in the first four generations of her pedigree. Such an ancestry would then strongly indicate that with so many unrelated progenitors, no gene could gain supremacy over another and that therefore an in-bred mating was required. In cases where the in-bred union has not produced the required traits expected, then the best of the resulting litter, providing that no major faults are apparent, would be mated to out-cross sires in an effort to hopefully eradicate the undesirable traits which the in-bred progeny had inherited. Moreover it would not be surprising if the litter resulting from the out-cross mating did not manifest the traits that the breeder had expected from the original in-bred mating.

If the chosen sire happens to be a Field Trial Champion, or, a Field Trial Winner, then well and good, but the field trial status of the sire must never take precedence over the blood ties governing inheritance.

Intent on building his bloodline, from each litter the breeder would select the best pup for his or her breeding programme. Contrary to popular belief, as a rule the breeder does not know which is the best pup, relying mainly on a gut hunch. Very often what may appear to be the best in the litter at eight weeks old, may turn out to be a duffer at six months old. Always allowing for the capriciousness of Mother Nature, it is by no means unusual for the breeder to have sold the 'star' of the litter that he has been searching for.

Advice

As I have said, not many breeders know how to recognise the 'star' of the litter, but the bitch does, for it is her favourite. For many years I employed a little trick as to how to be privy to that special information. The scheme is, when the pups are about four or five weeks old, lying comfortably with their mother in the warmth of the heat lamp, get someone to take the bitch for a short walk on the lead. As soon as you are alone with the pups, lift all of them from below the heat lamp and place them on the cold floor of the kennel. With a prearranged signal, your assistant outside will let the bitch off the lead. Stand back, for she will return at a gallop anxious to be re-united with her pups. Upon arrival and discovering that her pups have been removed from beneath the warmth of the heat lamp, she will frantically snuffle around each of her puppies on the cold floor. She will select a pup and replace it under the lamp: that is her favourite pup – and it is your first choice, for that is the 'star' of the litter. Mark it with a permanent marker pen. If you wish to keep more than one pup, then mark each of her choices in consecutive order.

As the breeder's experience develops through the years, he will notice frequently that as soon as the bitch has delivered her litter, not unusually, she will pick up one particular puppy and discard it. Should you replace this puppy she will repeatedly reject it. There is no point in getting sentimental and worrying about this, it is the law of nature. The bitch knows that there is no future for that pup and cannot afford to waste her milk on it.

(*see* Genetics page 53; Inheritance page 77; Lineage page 93; Line Breeding page 90; Out-cross Breeding, page 105)

Indiscriminate Breeding

In the sixties, seventies and the eighties, the trend in breeding dogs was to take the bitch to the popular dog of the moment, usually the Kennel Club Champion of the year, with scant regard as to whether there was a familial genetic link with which to justify the union. Whilst, in the main the results were not failures insofar as the breeder received more or less what he or she was looking for – puppies of a decent quality – the fly in the ointment was that in the next generation, that search for quality could never be repeated due to the random selection of sire. Sadly there seems little indication that anything has changed. The bitches are still being mated to the F.T. Champion of the moment, resulting in the ever growing genetical maelstrom of genes being thrown together with thousands of unrelated genes, each one independently trying to secure a place on the chromosome and thereby exert their influence, good or bad, upon the progeny.

By utilising in-breeding, line breeding, and out-cross breeding, with insight to the familial links recognised by perusing the pedigrees for related ancestry, a far more beneficial and systematic approach to breeding dogs can be achieved. It is only this approach to breeding that will ensure the bloodlines of the future.

Inheritance

The most immediate and greatest influence on the dog's genetical inheritance is brought about by judicious line breeding. As far as I am aware at this time of writing, sadly, there appears to be little evidence to support the idea that there are any bloodlines left pertaining to the working gundogs in the UK. I agree that this is a somewhat sweeping statement and I feel sure that if I am wrong in this assumption somebody out there is going to take great delight in metaphorically shooting me down in flames. I am also well aware that there is a proliferation of breeders who would like to think that they possess a bloodline, confusing such with a Kennel Club prefix.

Due to the breeders being more interested in how attractive the litter will appear to the public through the advertisements in the sporting press, the genetically inherited aspects are sometimes not considered. It is essential that some means of recognising the class animal is available and there is. If the breeder is in doubt, ignore the questionable champion and cast more than a quizzical eye on the dog who is consistently placed second or third.

The genes are what determine the total inherited bequest to the progeny from their antecedents. From this melting pot, activated at the exact moment of conception, all traits that contribute to making the individual character are formed. This is what determines uniquely every aspect of the individual dog, for no two dogs are completely alike. The genes and their genetical legacy gain their place on the chromosome at the time of conception and from that instant the dye is irrevocably cast: it cannot be altered – therein lies the miracle of life itself. Each puppy in the litter receives an equal share of genes, but not exactly the same mix. It is because of this that when we look at human brothers and sisters, the family resemblance may be quite striking yet individual family members are not exactly the same. In related parents, these genes would be (homozygous) familial genes and as such they would seek out and unite with their familial ilk donated by their immediate ancestry. In this way they have an advantage over the unrelated genes and can thereby become dominant. The unrelated genes are still on the chromosome however, albeit hidden but ever ready to unite when the opportunity arises through future matings. It is directly attributable to these subservient genes lying dormant for generation after generation concealing a fault, that, to the great surprise and mystification of the breeders the fault suddenly appears in a litter. The genes would have united with one of their ilk, gaining dominance and manifesting an undesirable trait, where no such fault apparently existed before.

We know the percentages that the progeny's parents, grandparents, etc. donate to the genetic legacy of their progeny. It would be tempting to deduce

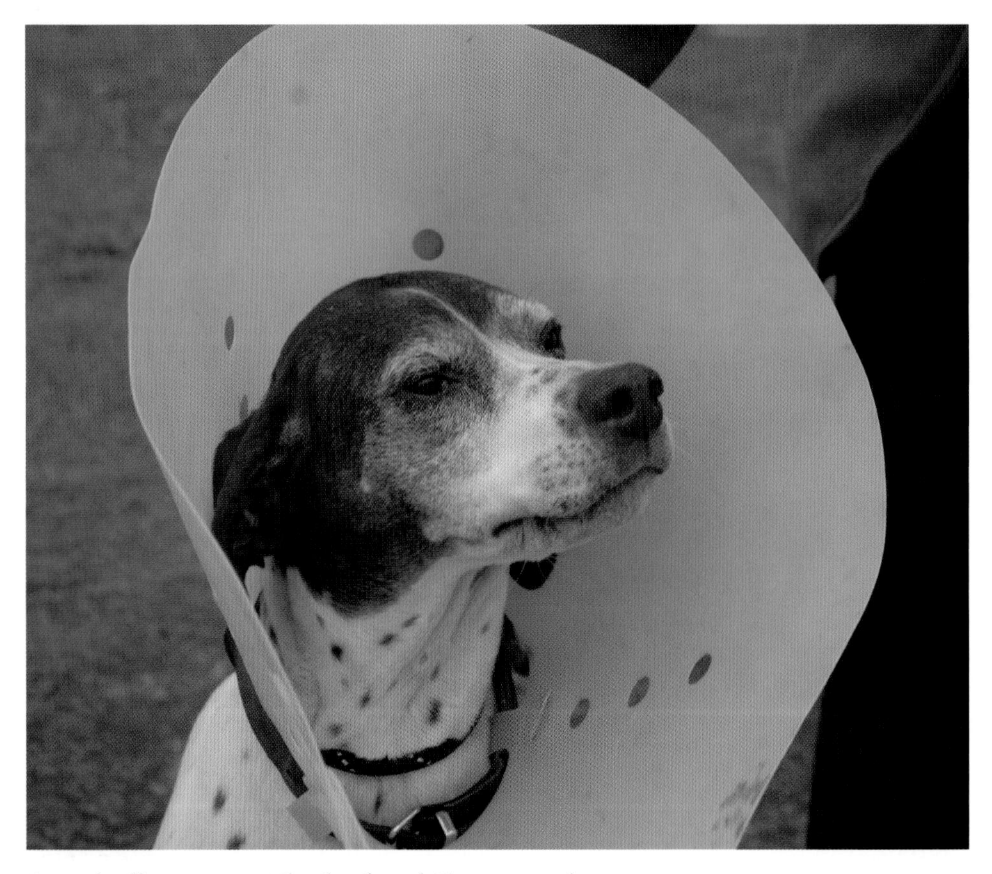

A good collar to prevent the dog from biting a wound.

A common problem for spaniels is to get seeds in their ears.

that the pup's sire and dam were the principal donors to their litter's genetic legacy. Such is not the case however, for it is the grandparents that are the main donors to the progeny's genetic inheritance, the parents acting merely as a genetic vehicle. Even with a first-class breeding programme, carefully selecting only top class animals, nothing can be guaranteed. How many times have we, the breeders of gundogs, after mating animals who were apparently fault-free, been convinced that this time, we were about to receive all the good traits that we were striving for, only to be disappointed? Yet after mating with one of the offspring, the very traits that we were so hopeful of procuring from their parents manifested themselves.

Injuries

I have often been asked by my clients how to prevent a dog biting at an injury after veterinary treatment.

Advice

The best way to avoid this is simply to adapt a plastic bucket, by cutting out a hole in the bottom through which to insert the dog's head. Next cut from the top lip of the bucket all the way down one side to the hole in the bottom.

Lastly, bore eye-holes all the way round the bottom of the bucket. (A heated metal knitting needle is ideal for this.) Through the eye holes thread a plastic cord, looping it round the dog's collar and then tie it off. You may then, by opening the side of the bucket, allow the dog's head through the hole at the bottom of the bucket then fasten the already secured collar. It does not look pretty but it does the job.

Chapter Ten

J

Judges and Judging

It cannot be disputed that the most important governing factor in field trials lies in the degree of honesty and efficiency of the judges. One can ask no more than the judges do their best in being fair with their decisions and regarding all competitors without fear or favour. Of course judges can make a mistake and they cannot be blamed for doing so. In the words of Albert Einstein, 'He who never made a mistake, never made anything.' In time the honest judge will become easily recognised.

The novice gundog trainer will after he has trained a dog and competed in trials with some success, be asked to judge a trial. In accepting the nomination you the novice judge, would do well to give some thought to the competitors. By attending the trial these people have placed their trust in you. Many will have travelled a considerable distance at no small expense in fuel and hotel fees. These people are entitled to a fair deal, no matter how persuasive anyone else may be in trying to influence your decision. It was you who saw the dog performing and it is you who should make the decision.

Your responsibilities do not end there though, for not only will you be judging your peers, your decisions will also affect the professional handlers who will be running dogs in front of you. Remember this, the professional is not in the field trial game for a hobby nor for an image. He does it for a living; the field trials are his shop window; it is from these that the public will judge his expertise. I am not aware of any other profession where a man's living is so directly affected by the actions of amateurs.

There is nothing difficult in judging a field trial. Besides yourself there will be the other judge, a referee, probably two game carriers, one at each side of the line, a trial steward who tries to keep the spectators grouped at the end of the line and who will call up the dogs for your attention in numerical order.

First and foremost, the novice judge must be fully conversant with the Kennel Club field trial rules. During the trial you will be called upon to handle all the game retrieved by the dog which is under your scrutiny at that point in time. You must therefore be skilled in recognising 'hard mouth' for you will be required to examine each head of game before putting it into the game carrier's bag. If you are not familiar with the technique then seek instruction from someone who is. When in doubt you must confer with the other judge and occasionally the referee as arbitrator.

The dogs competing will all be numbered: the odd numbers will go under the senior judge on the right side of the line, and the even numbers under the junior judge on the left of the line. Most judges score a trial in the same way. At the beginning of the trial you will be given a book in which all the dogs are listed with their numbers. It is not required that the judge make lengthy notes regarding each dog, in fact rather than clarifying the issue you could wind up thoroughly confused. It is far handier, just to make little abbreviated notes or alphabetical codes such as PD 'poor delivery', GD 'good delivery', GH 'good hunter', GGF 'good game finder', GR 'good retrieve', PR 'poor retrieve', EW 'eye wipe' -1-2-3 i.e. first, second or third dog tried, FR 'failed retrieve', U 'unsteady', NH 'noisy handling' etc. These are a few examples that I have used. No doubt as your experience grows, you will develop your own style.

I never judged a trial as a fault finder, nevertheless faults are committed and must be penalised. Hard mouth, giving tongue, running in, pegging game and refusing to 'leave it', missing or blinking game, noisy handling, and whilst it will not be dealt with too severely in a novice stake, the dog that lays down game in an open stake must never figure in the awards. These are all pretty obvious, but there are controversial or grey areas. For instance on ground game I would view severely the handler who was resorting to whistle and hand-signalling to direct his dog onto ground game, even if the game had been shot to the other dog and had been given to a competitor for a retrieve, for there is no excuse. Any dog worth his keep should be able to take a line. A bird falling unseen by the dog is an entirely different matter.

Usually during the trial, you may see the dog at the other side of the line flush a bird. Not unusually, your fellow judge may decide that the dog in front of him has had sufficient retrieves, in which case he may call down to you to see if your dog could use the retrieve. In such a circumstance you will be required to take your competitor with his dog up the back of the line to where the other dog had flushed the bird. Your competitor may or may not decide to put his dog on the lead. As it is a hunting dog however, he would be wise to do so and technically as he is not strictly speaking in the line, you cannot penalise him for doing so. I have seen more than one trial list disqualified because in passing over ground that his dog had already hunted with the dog walking free at heel, it suddenly darted out and flushed game.

At lunchtime you and your fellow judge may compare notes regarding which dogs have impressed each of you in the morning. At or around lunchtime, depending on how things have progressed in the morning, the even-numbered dogs and the odd-numbered dogs will change so that all dogs will have appeared under both judges by the end of the trial.

Judges comparing notes.

Once all the dogs have competed, the judges will then consult as to which dogs in each of their opinions had been the most impressive. It is rare that both judges would be in complete agreement, therefore more often than not a run-off will be required. In a retriever trial in the run-off the emphasis will be on retrieving. On the other hand in the spaniel trial, the most important deciding factor for the judges will be in making a final comparison in the performance in hunting pertaining to ground treatment, speed and style by each dog. These dogs in the run-off are the judges' final choices from the main trial, but are not necessarily the winner, for it may be that one dog has shone far above the others and is on what is termed the 'shelf'; that is he does not appear in the run-off. In my opinion, having been satisfied in the body of the stake all that I would be looking for in the run-off would be the dogs that looked as though they were the game finders.

Jumping (General Training)

Most gundogs are natural jumpers, only requiring to be shown before they will involve themselves with alacrity. I have never experienced any difficulty in teaching a dog to jump, if 'teaching' could be the right word for I never really made a big thing out of it. As with all training, I merely adapted or utilised the changing situations that presented themselves each day. Consequently, I would clamber over a wall – of which there were plenty in my locality – and let the dog struggle over it. The dog then could be said to be learning by example.

Ideally, the dog's introduction to jumping should be by example and despite what I have already said regarding the 'schoolmaster' dog, just as with swimming this is another learning pursuit where I may utilise the older dog. Not every gundog owner has access to another dog however and therefore the trainer has no option but to set the example personally. This is no great problem; it merely means the trainer hopping over the 'jump' and then encouraging the pup to surmount the obstacle too.

Initially the 'jumps' should be low and preferably wooden which enables the pup to gain a foothold on the top; in other words, 'cat-jump', which many pups will do until they gain confidence. These wooden obstacles must gradually increase in size as time goes on and the dog gains in physique, thus providing a more challenging obstacle for him to jump as he gains confidence. As soon as the pup has proven that these jumps no longer present a challenge to him, then the introduction to fence jumping will be initiated. Again, just as with the wooden jumps, the wire fence jumps start off low and progressively get more challenging. Under no circumstances however, would I ever encourage a dog to jump barbed wire fences.

Once the dog has become skilled in jumping, the trainer will initiate the dog to retrieve over jumps. This of course should not prove difficult. The only difference from the conventional retrieving will be to send the dog for the retrieve, then to call him to halt by whistle before he reaches the jump. The trainer would then walk forward, stop briefly, then give the command 'Over', and immediately 'Hup' the dog on the other side momentarily, before sending him to complete the retrieve. At first glance this may seem all a trifle unnecessary. It is not. The trainer is illustrating to the dog that he must stop at any obstacle and wait for the command before surmounting it. As with all training the dog must not be aware that he is being schooled, in other words, make it into a fun game.

Later, once the dog is performing in the shooting field, a slight problem may be encountered with his first few retrieves, perhaps as he tries to negotiate a fence or a wall with the unaccustomed weight of a cock bird or a hare. I am content if he manages to deliver the game to me; style will develop with experience. I would most certainly not engage in any kind of cajoling whilst a dog is retrieving, for in doing so all that will be achieved will be to display to the dog that something is amiss. As dogs always associate your reaction with their last action, in this case retrieving, you will only create more problems regarding retrieving.

I am a great believer in being thankful for small mercies, and after all there is always tomorrow. Nothing can teach like experience and so, if he has been retrieving the dummy adequately in the jumping exercises without the added weight of the bird, don't worry about it. All will come right in the end.

(*see* Creative Imagination page 22)

Chapter Eleven

K

Kennels – Reluctance to Return To

This is very common especially in the young puppy during his 'humanisation' period and is, to put it quite simply, the puppy making a statement. He is saying, I've been in here before and it's pretty boring, why should I go in there when I'm having such fun out here? In the well-trained dog of course, this, as a rule does not happen, except in exceptional circumstances and of course there is always a reason, but it is up to the trainer to recognise it.

During an exceptionally busy period in kennels, involving a great deal of rigorous cleaning and disinfecting of kennels together with dogs coming into and dogs going home, a set of circumstances came to my attention which in the normal course of events might well have gone unnoticed. On two or three occasions over a period of approximately two weeks, several kennel assistants reported to me of difficulties they were having in kennelling new dogs. In commercial kennels it is always a good idea to have at least one spare dry kennel in which to house an unexpected arrival, or just to house one of the residents who for one reason or another needs to be kennelled alone. It was reported to me that none of the newcomers would enter one specific kennel and no amount of persuasion was going to work whereby the new dog would be comfortable in that kennel. When asked which dog was the last resident a long-held theory of mine was at last confirmed.

It is a commonly held view that various different canine packs, such as the wolves, or every group of dogs, has a leader – the 'top dog'. I was well aware that Macsiccar Kennels had its long-resident master of the pack, Macsiccar Cherokee. My theory was relating to scent. Could a dog differentiate between the ranks of the opposition by scent, and furthermore could he recognise rank and threat also?

Various authorities down through the years have recognised that the scenting powers of the dog are far in excess of ours. It doesn't take much intelligence to come to that conclusion. One authority holds the view that the dog is capable of recognising a scent buried for three thousand years. As I have no idea how these conclusions are reached, I am not prepared to argue with them, being quite content in the inescapable knowledge that their scenting powers are many times greater than ours.

Being slap bang in the middle of hunting country, the kennels were plagued nightly by foxes. Their presence each night was greeted by a resounding cacophony from the outdoor kennels. Without fail, after only a few minutes, one bark from Cherokee, who liked his sleep, was sufficient to silence the rest.

As it was revealed to me that the last dog to reside in the kennel in question was Macsiccar Cherokee, it appears that my theory was correct. Dogs could recognise the status of another by scent, despite the copious disinfecting and instinctively recognise the threat. The fact that the kennel was empty did nothing to allay that fear and consequently they were reluctant to enter that kennel.

Kennel Sickness

This is thankfully a comparatively rare condition, one that I associate closely with the human neurosis of reactive depression. This must not be confused with the stage in training when most puppies no matter how bold will go through a withdrawn period. In the male it can happen at any time, however with the female it can be expected at or around her first season.

Advice

The cause may simply be that the dog, besieged with all these new commands in training, loses confidence. The cure is simply to give the dog a couple of weeks' rest from training. It will do him no harm and in all probability, solve the problem.

In the professional gun dog training establishment, kennel sickness, although rare, is more common than in the one man one dog situation. Where the owner has only the training and care of one dog, to allow this condition to manifest itself in the first place is inexcusable, for it would suggest that the dog and its welfare had been sorely neglected. On the other hand, such a condition can manifest itself very easily in the professional kennels due to excessive demands placed on the trainer's time in training his clients' pups and should only occur in his own dogs, never the client's.

As the name 'reactive depression' suggests, the condition is a reaction to a particular set of circumstances. Because the dog neither expects, nor requires much from life, the recognition of the sickness and its solution / treatment is much more obvious and therefore simplified. In general it is simply lack of attention, the condition once known as 'pining'. In the human whose expectations and aspirations from life are much greater than the dog, the diagnosis and subsequent treatment is much more complicated.

The first signs or symptoms are displayed when the dog's kennel is approached and the dog is allowed out, but he does not look happy and displays the 'hangdog' look: his head down, a crouching gait with a slight arch of the back, and his tail between his legs. Once noticed, the daily kennel routine pertaining to that dog must be drastically altered. Always upon arriving at the kennels, the trainer must make a point of stopping off at that particular dog's kennel, speaking to him, or, better still, taking a few moments to open his kennel and go into the run and make a fuss of him, even though he does not plan to take him out of kennel at that particular time.

Advice

The curative treatment is simplicity itself. Just put the bounce back into him. Get him out as often as possible and put any training thoughts out of your mind. With the minimum of control, allow him to run and enjoy your company. If the condition appears to be very severe, you may consider that a spell of chasing a few rabbits would be indicated.* Once a few days have passed and you see that his tail is up and the 'hangdog' look has gone will be soon enough to contemplate reinstating a training regime.

(**see* Neurotic Aversion to Scent – Page 100)

Know-How

As a rule, the professional trainer will require his clients to enter their dogs for training with him at six months of age. Moreover, they will have informed the client that they will require the dog to be only minimally trained, in other words, only in the basic training such as coming to vocal or whistle command.

With the professional trainer's own dogs, it is by no means unusual for their training not to commence until eleven or twelve months old, in some cases even later, for a more immature dog. I have had many friends who started their dogs as late as eighteen months old. Why the urgency then to take in your pup for training? It is to get it away from you before you ruin the dog's potential. This may appear rather a cruel thing to say, but it is the truth. The professional trainer knows from experience that even at such a tender age, he will be able to train the pup, whereas the amateur trainer is more than likely to ruin its chances.

The most common reason for the amateur's failure in training his dog is, quite simply, his or her eagerness and impatience to press on regardless, commencing the next step in the pup's tuition as soon as it looks as though he has absorbed the current lesson. So what can be wrong? Why is it that with so many good books, even videos, with all that guidance available, why can the amateur not succeed? I think that I stumbled on the answer a long time ago, when I first introduced the *Gundog Training Correspondence Course*. All the books and all the videos in the world, however well-written or produced, will never prevent the amateur trainer from charging on, regardless even of giving the training sequence in the wrong order, because that bit in the book looks far more interesting than the part that we have reached at the moment. The problems are inevitable.

Thinking about this, it becomes apparent that what the reader requires in conjunction with the written word is further guidance. A sequence of training to be laid out in such a fashion as to control the reader's enthusiasm

'Hup' – group attention is desirable. The author with a group of springers in his heyday.

and place each segment of the training in its proper place. Consequently, I am including the 'know-how', in the form of a training plan – an aspect of the training manual never attempted before.

The first note of caution must be to emphasise most strongly that the training of your dog is not a race. It does not matter how well your friend's dog appears to be progressing, for all you know he may be riding for a fall. Each dog is different, even within the litter a marked difference can be noticed in the individual dog's rate of absorption as compared with its siblings. Moreover, it is not at all unusual for a dog that up to a certain point appears to have been taking all its training in its stride, suddenly, for no apparent reason to manifest all kinds of problems. In all probability what has happened is that his trainer has taken the training step by step, quite correctly, however has progressed through the training too rapidly resulting in the young dog's brain being overloaded, and consequently a type of burn-out occurs. On the other hand it can be the result of initiating some lessons in the wrong order, resulting in the amateur's dog becoming confused. The golden rule must always be, make haste slowly.

I am reasonably confident that between the ages of eight weeks and six months, providing that the children have not been allowed to throw dummies for the dog to endlessly retrieve, problems should not arise. It is from six months on that the trainer must be on guard.

Chapter Twelve

L

Leave It! (Early Training)

This is one of the most valuable commands that can be taught to a dog and is the precursor to the more advanced training yet to come, for obviously a dog that will ignore a dead bird that he has marked and handled on to an unmarked bird that is down and running, is worth his weight in gold.

From his earliest days as a puppy, whenever the trainer notices him at his daily scamper around 'pottering' or just stopping to examine some object, animal droppings, anything that is not required by the handler, the opportunity is taken to command him with a stern tone to 'Leave it', accompanied by a motion of the hand to indicate to him that you wish him to move on. It may be that the scent or whatever is distracting the puppy is too strong a temptation and the puppy, because he does not as yet recognise this new command, does not comply, in which case, the handler will crouch down, clap his hands and with the plastic pea-less whistle, give two 'peep-peeps' to encourage him to return and as he does, with a sideways motion of the hand, tell him 'Leave It – Gone Away!' It will not be too long before he will recognise what the trainer requires from him. As with all commands given to the dog in his puppy days, by the time he has matured, it will be second nature for him to obey without question.

Line Breeding

Down through the ages, countless authors make reference to the breeding of dogs, few if *any* deal with it in detail, content to make apparently knowledgeable observations, but never dealing with the 'nuts and bolts' of the subject. It is almost as though they were afraid to commit themselves.

Rather than blindly accepting the opinions of others I suggest that the breeders would enjoy greater success by creating a genuine bloodline of their own. By implementing some thought to the relationship of the stud dogs to that of the bitches, a consistent blood line can be built up which inevitably must lead to the improvement of the breed.

Repeatedly choosing an unrelated sire because he happens to be a field trial champion, achieves nothing. The breeder is only dipping his hand into a veritable genetic Pandora's box, for there is no conceivable way of knowing what the results will be. If continued to excess all that the breeder will achieve is total fragmentation in the gene pool, no genes being in the state where they can gain supremacy over the other.

There is nothing weird or wonderful about line breeding. If my reader accepts my theory that the strength of a kennel lies in the quality of its bitches, then the following system of breeding relates to the female line. For the first mating to a particular bitch, after scrutiny of the sire and dam's pedigrees and determining that there were close familial links to one another, the breeder would implement the mating which would, through the union of the homologous familial genes be line-bred. In the fullness of time when choosing a sire for the line bred progeny, the breeder would choose a sire

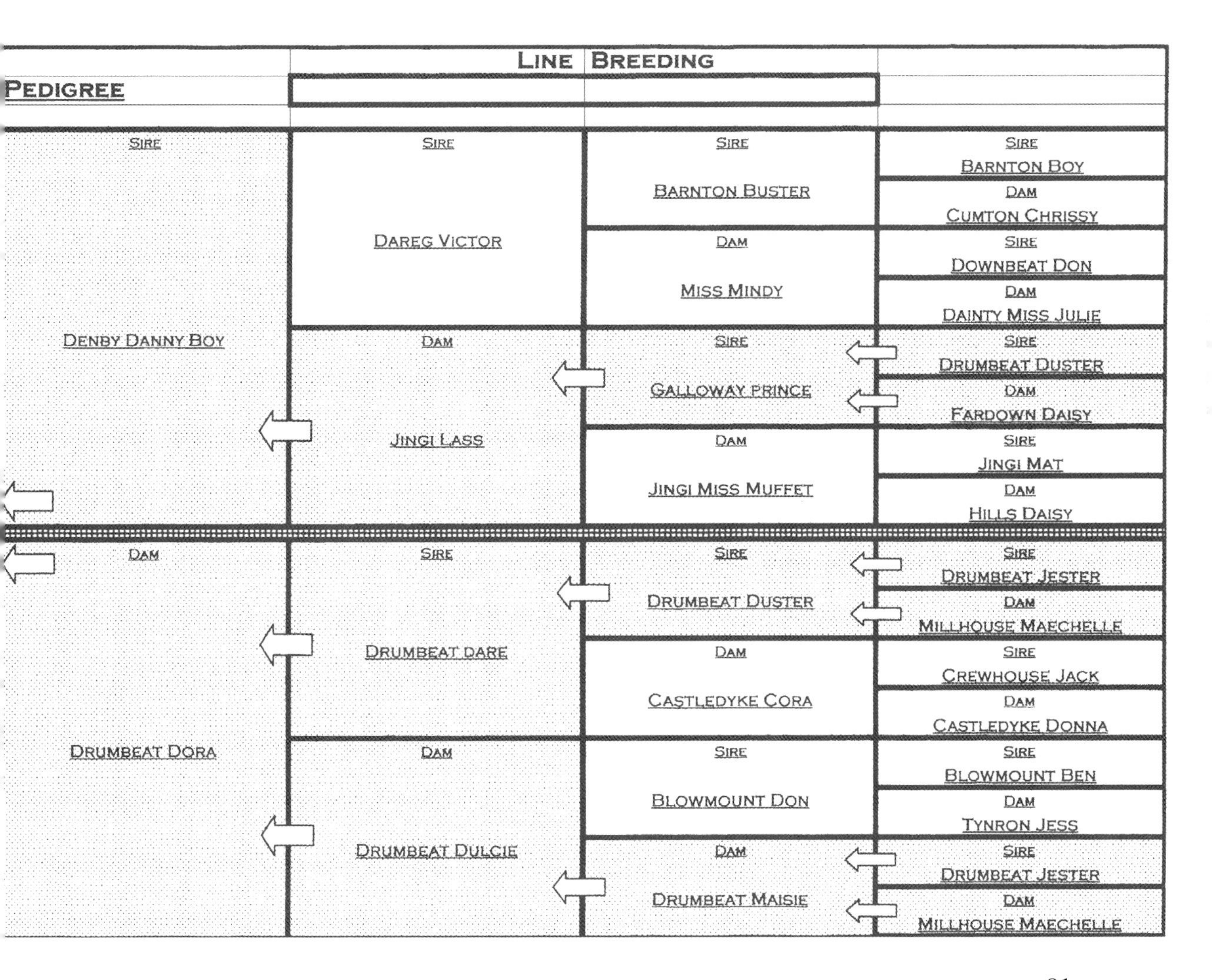

who was related to the bitch within the grandparents or the great grandparents. Again in due course, a female progeny from that union, would be mated to an unrelated sire thereby constituting the outcross mating. The progeny from these three matings would be the first step to the breeder acquiring a bloodline.

Logistically Unsafe?

Whether those who propound the notion that the dog is the most influential genetic force, like it or not, in my experience the evidence clearly indicates that the strongest genetic influence is through the dam line. Occasionally, and in my view by pure chance, a mating from an inferior bitch may result in producing a litter within which one or two puppies appear to be of a superior class to their siblings. I say 'appear to be of a superior class', for it must not be forgotten that these puppies, as well as their brothers and sisters, are the holders of recessive genes which may appear at any time in the future progeny if the recessive gene is unknowingly reinforced with a genetical (homozygous) familial match. Nevertheless a poor bitch, no matter how good the sire may be, will generally produce only poor puppies. There can be no wiser maxim adopted for breeding than 'one fault is one fault too many'. Consequently if the breeder is aware that his bitch has a fault, he must consider carefully as to whether or not, she is worth breeding from.

As I have said many times in the past, anyone who decides to breed from a bitch takes on a responsibility to the breed concerned. For by breeding dogs, he or she sets in motion an irreversible chain of genetic inheritance for the rest of time. This should be a sobering thought. However, it seems that little or no consideration is ever apportioned to the seriousness of the breeder's responsibility. This is not to suggest, that some weighty tome of responsibility is poised like the sword of Damocles over the head of the breeder, it simply means that if you are compelled for whatever reason to breed dogs, then you must embark upon it in a responsible manner.

Where are the bloodlines such as the 'Rivington', 'Saighton' and 'Ovara', to name but a few of yesteryear, or even their contemporary counterparts? Sadly they appear to have gone. In saying that, I hasten to add that out there somewhere, there may be a few enlightened breeders quietly working away building their bloodline. I hope there are; it is merely that at present I am unaware of them. There is a great deal of evidence to suggest that the majority of those who indulge in the breeding of dogs just do not have the knowledge required to read a pedigree or to understand even the most rudimentary principles pertaining to genetics.

In their eagerness to produce quality progeny but not possessing the knowledge as to how best to go about it and lacking confidence in their own judgement, many present-day breeders depend upon the decisions made by field trial judges as to what is quality or not. In choosing sires haphazardly, simply because they are field trial champions, without due regard as to whether they are related or not to the bitch, the resulting pedigrees can

resemble a Pandora's box, a system with neither rhyme nor reason behind it. For either the pedigree indicated that the dogs in the first three generations were totally unrelated – an outcross – or showed over in-breeding. Very rarely indeed have I come across a pedigree that showed sensible line breeding, which is the staff of life for breeding purposes.
(*see* figure page 91; Line Breeding page 90)

Lineage

Unlike most stud dog owners, I have never subscribed to the belief that the dominant genetic influence stems from the sire, for I am firmly of the opinion that a kennel is only as strong as its bitches, that is to say, the dam line is the source of the greatest genetic influence on the resulting progeny. If the breeder is the owner of a top-class bitch, one that he cannot see a fault in, then he is fortunate, for he has the choice of every top-class dog in the country from whom to choose a sire. In the event that the bitch owner's selection of a sire proves to be disappointing, little damage may be done to the resulting progeny, since the sire can only maintain the quality in the offspring; it rarely if ever supplements it.

Conversely, if a kennel only has second-class bitches, then they are at a distinct disadvantage, for mating these bitches to any amount of top-class sires will be of little avail, for in the main only second-class progeny will result. It is possible from time to time for a substandard bitch to produce one or two puppies of superior quality to herself, however this is just by chance and as a rule will not repeat itself.

There are those who claim that the dog is the mainstay of any breeding policy, that there are prepotent sires who will 'stamp their likeness upon the breed'. As far as I am concerned such assertions cannot hold any credence, for if such were to be the case, then surely the owner of a second-class bitch would only require to mate the bitch to one of these stallions of the breed and 'Hey Presto' no more second-class pups. If only it were so simple.

Lining Ground Scent (General Training)

This is the term used to refer to a dog pulling away out in front of the handler, when instead of hunting within his usual ground treatment he breaks off his regular pattern and heads off nose down on a footscent to the extent that he will eventually be hunting out of shot. It is a most undesirable trait and one that must be stopped as soon as it is noticed by the trainer. This habit relates to the dog's scenting capabilities, the better his nose the more likely he is to indulge in this and he may even appear to his handler to become whistle deaf, if the handler is experiencing a great deal of trouble in commanding the dog's attention, then it is most probable that his dog is a bold outgoing character, headstrong and with an excellent nose. I have had dogs in for training whose scenting capabilities were so poor that it would not be difficult to believe that they couldn't have found their dinner in the middle of a concrete path. Such dogs will never develop a tendency to 'line' ground scent.

There are many causes that may contribute to a dog habitually lining ground scent. As I have said, it may be that your dog is quite simply a head-strong character with a very good nose, who may present many problems throughout his training. Very commonly, lining may be attributed to the handler skimping on the dog's earlier training with regard to his coming back to the return whistle. On the other hand it may simply be that you have introduced him to scent-holding ground too soon, before you have managed to make his ground treatment tuition secure. Consequently, as soon as the immature dog encounters strong scent he will break away from his regular hunting pattern and pursue the line.

He may have acquired the fault very early in his puppyhood days by being allowed free hunting along the hedgerows (*see* Dashing along the Hedgerows page 25). Lining ground scent might also suggest that at some time in the past he had encountered game and chased it, thus he has remembered the scent and the creature associated with it. One redeeming factor is that dogs who tend to be 'liners' very rarely become 'sticky' with their hunting, for they tend to be the type of dog that 'hots up'. Finally, humbling though it may be, lining footscent and ignoring his trainer's commands might simply be that he has no respect for his handler.

Advice

Dogs that fall into the habit of lining ground scent are obviously over orientated to scent. The trainer must therefore prevent the dog from hunting on ground that contains scent, until such times as he has instilled complete compliance to the whistle commands pertaining to his ground treatment. Finding scent-fallow ground may not be as easy as one would imagine, but find it you must.

There are dogs that just will not hunt on scentless ground, being too intelligent. If your dog shows a tendency not to quarter on scent-free ground, yet hots up on encountering scent, then there is only one option left to you. The handler must clear game from the chosen training venue. Forewarned is forearmed and in the knowledge that he is going to line ground scent, you will be ready to take remedial actions.

Remember in training the working dog, if any success is to be achieved there must always be the ultimate deterrent – the 'thunderer' stop whistle. This is the whistle that must never, under any circumstances be disobeyed. Before embarking upon the following regime, if you are in any doubt as to his obedience relating to the stop whistle, you must abandon proceeding further until such times as you are confident of complete compliance from the dog.

Dealing with a habitual 'liner' is a situation that demands stern measures. You must show the dog that this will not be tolerated. As soon as he breaks from his hunting pattern, gets his nose to the ground and begins to line out on footscent, you must give him the return whistle command. There is every likelihood that he will be so engrossed with the scent that he will ignore it – that is your signal. Immediately, drop him to the stop whistle and don't forget; short and sharp signals. If he drops and he should – for, if he doesn't, then you must realise that you really do have a problem. Obviously you have not instilled sufficient obedience to the stop whistle in him. The trainer in such a situation must face up to the fact that if he cannot get obedience to the stop whistle in the mildly tempting situation regarding lining on ground scent, then he doesn't stand a chance of getting obedience to the stop whistle in the much more tempting future situation, when the dog encounters and flushes game for the first time. A refresher course in dropping to the stop whistle is obviously required.

If on the other hand the dog has obeyed the stop whistle command, the trainer has then commanded the dog's attention. Pause, allow him time to collect his thoughts, then, crouch down to one side and with a mid-air patting motion near the ground, give him the recall whistle signal and as he makes his way back, swing him off to one side or the other with the turn whistle

The Downwind Beat

If he tends to 'pull out' too far, recall him with the double 'peep-peep' signal accompanied by a 'patting motion' of the hand, indicating that you wish him to work closer to that side.

and hand signal. Providing this aspect of training is adhered to relentlessly, then the problem of lining footscent will be solved.

In time the trainer must bite the bullet and present his dog to game-holding ground. In the knowledge that he has been guilty of lining out on footscent in the past, the fact that he has apparently been successfully 'cured' of this complaint means nothing. He is not yet worthy of the trainer's trust. The handler must always play safe with a young dog; carelessness will usually bring disappointment. Play safe rather than be sorry. This is one of these situations where the handler must decide what his role is in training the dog. He must, if any hope of success is to be envisaged, play the role of gundog trainer first and rough shooter second. It is imperative therefore that the handler leaves his gun at home for the time being.

Equipped with a starter pistol and a couple of dummies the handler will hunt the dog and be alert. The dog's body language, even with a young inexperienced dog, will indicate when he is working onto good scent. Be ready. As soon as he has flushed the game, blast the stop whistle. Fire the pistol. He must obey or it's back to the refresher course in dropping to the stop whistle and shot. Remember, the stop whistle is the ultimate deterrent. If he has dropped to the whistle and or pistol, wait for about a minute and then, in full view of him, chuck a dummy in the opposite direction to that taken by the game. After a pause send him for it. Assuming that he retrieves the dummy successfully, and there is no reason to believe otherwise for it is a simple exercise, hunt him on. If he flushes game, stop him with the whistle, fire the pistol, pause, then this time with a distinctive hand signal, recommence his hunting by giving him the verbal command 'Get On' and with a distinct clear hand signal wave him on in the opposite direction to that which the game has taken. Very often, especially with a young inexperienced dog, he will attempt to take the line of the game. Stop him immediately, order him, 'No –Leave It' or 'No – Gone Away' and again send him hunting in the opposite direction.

(*see* Drop – Disobedience To page 33; Disobeying the Return Whistle page 31)

Chapter Thirteen

M

Mistakes

It is probably the most aggravating and frustrating aspect of dog training to find that in spite of giving the client lengthy intensive demonstrations and instructions on handling his dog at the completion of six months' training, that within a few weeks, the dog would be brought back as 'useless'. Often the failure is not as the client would wish the trainer to believe, the fault of the dog or the trainer. It is directly due to the client's mistakes caused by not listening to the trainer's instructions.

The most common complaint is that after only a few weeks the dog was 'running into shot'. In other words, every time a shot was fired the dog was off into the wide blue yonder, without waiting for instruction from his handler. Upon being questioned the client might admit, 'yes' he had been sending the dog for every bird shot. When asked if he remembered my stressing to him that during the dog's first season, he should only be allowed to pick every other bird, and then, only after an appreciable pause, 'No' would be the answer. In other words, he had not been listening. Depending on how long the dog had been away from kennels, the amount of re-integration he would or would not require would depend on how long it would take to effect a cure.

Advice

There is no mystery to this cure if we remember that the dog learns by association, and we act accordingly. Because he has learned to 'run into shot' by the wrong association – the report of the gun and the immediate order to 'fetch it', the dog has to be re-educated to wait for the command before setting out to retrieve. In other words, the trainer is required to reverse the process of association.

The dog is taken to a suitable spot and told to 'Hup!' The trainer then steps a few paces away and fires off the dummy launcher at an angle away from the dog. (Never discharge a dummy launcher or a shotgun from behind a dog at close quarters, for in doing so the dog will receive the full blast of the report.) Now the dog may run into the report or not. If he doesn't, that is a good sign for it tells you that the dog has not completely forgotten you and remembers that you will not tolerate such behaviour. If he runs in, then just let him bring back the dummy, don't make a big thing out of the incident, reload the dummy launcher, with the dummy only partly down the spigot, for it is you who will be doing the retrieving and you don't want to be walking too far. Once again discharge the launcher and immediately cry 'Hup', raising your arm to the upright signal even if it means getting between the dog and the fallen dummy. Once you are sure that he is sitting steadily, walk out, pick up the dummy, return to him and quietly praise him. You may repeat this procedure two or three times before allowing him one retrieve before returning him to kennels. Between giving him a little hunt every day, for you would bore the dog to tears if every day you confined his activities purely to sitting watching you firing the dummy launcher, you would finish his exercise with the steadiness to shot regime. Usually, the dog will have reverted back to his original training in respect to the shot within around three weeks. Hopefully the client will have learned his lesson.

I remember one warm spring morning I was in the process of re-introducing a canine miscreant in the ways of steadiness to the shot. I had discharged the dummy launcher a couple of times and retrieved the dummy myself, when I began to have a sensation that I was being watched. I shrugged the feeling off, and had just walked out for the fourth time to pick up the dummy, when the feeling became very powerful. I scanned the nearby thick hawthorn hedge. It seemed solid, but at one point where there was a slight dip in height, I met someone's eye. Upon realising that I had seen him, he grunted the customary Scots greeting.

'Aye,' he said, 'It's a grand day. Are you doing a bit of dog training?'

'Yes,' I replied.

'Ahuh! Well, that's a bonny looking wee dog you've got there, but it's him that should be doing the retrieving though,' he said, as he departed with a smug little smile.

Another common mistake is to endlessly send the dog for dummies lying out on bare ground, over and over again. Nothing will put a dog off retrieving faster than that. Another error is expecting too much from a young dog, perhaps by presenting him with a retrieve, far and away too complicated for his young shoulders. 'Make haste slowly', 'all in good time', 'implement training in easy steps' and 'make sure each step has been thoroughly bedded into the dog's consciousness, before attempting the next lesson' – all are wise dictums to be adhered to in dog training.

I remember one of my clients turned up at the kennels one day and on getting out of his car his first words were, 'I'm sorry, Joe, but this damned dog isn't worth a light. She won't do a thing that I tell her.'

My reply was, 'Well it's your fault, not the dog's. She's a field trial winner, so she is most certainly worth a damn sight more than a light. Get her out of the car please.' As soon as she was out of the car she took a flying dive at me, excitedly jumping up and down, obviously having recognised me.

'Let's get her down into the woods,' I said, 'then we'll see what she has been up to.'

Upon reaching the woods, my client turned to me asking, 'Will you require my whistles?'

'No, I won't be working her, you will. I want to see what she has been doing with you,' I replied.

Rather self-consciously he cast her off, then for the next four or five minutes he kept turning to me, with, 'I'm sorry, Joe, I swear to you she's never worked like this for me from the moment I took her home.'

The bitch was giving a copybook performance. After a short time I decided to put him out of his misery. 'There's nothing wrong with her, but there's something gone wrong with her post-training experience. It's as simple as that. She's just got out of your car, spotted and remembered me so she will not do any wrong today. Your mistake is, you're too nice a man and she knows it!'

We returned to the kennels, she was put into the back of my car and we departed for one of my training grounds. For the rest of the morning I once more demonstrated for him every aspect of her training and stressed to him that he must treat her as I treat her. He was not to be lazy and let her get away with anything, and hopefully everything would work out in the end. He kept in touch for many years but when I left Lockerbie sadly we lost touch.

Chapter Fourteen

N

The enlightened gundog trainer will be aware that as a dog is conditioned by pleasant association, that equally he can be averted by unpleasant association and the trainer must guard against it. The following anecdote represents a classic case of what not to do.

Neurotic Aversion to Scent

Many years ago I remember receiving a telephone call from a trainer who lived in the north of Scotland.

'Hello Joe, would you like to buy a golden cocker? I've got one here; you can have her for a hundred pounds. Thing is,' he continued 'she won't hunt!'

I asked him why I would want to purchase a bitch that wouldn't hunt.

'Well I was talking to so-and-so the other day,' he replied, 'and he reckoned that nobody but you could train her.' I refused his offer.

'I'll tell you what then,' he persisted, 'I'll let you have her for nothing. If you manage to train her, you can pay me the money, but if you don't manage to train her, just shoot her.'

After informing him that I was not in the business of shooting dogs and that if I didn't manage to train her successfully, I would find a good home for her and he would get nothing, I arranged to go to his house the following weekend. When I arrived he took me out to his kennels. There was the most gorgeous little cocker bitch of seven months old.

The trainer opened the kennel gate and the poor wee thing slithered out of the kennel on her belly dragging her back legs behind her, obviously terrified of something. He put a lead on her and literally dragged her out to an open space at the back of the kennels. The little cocker just sat there in front of him quivering with fear.

'Get on – Get on' he said impatiently, but she didn't move. Suddenly, before I realised what he was going to do, he raised his shepherd's crook and gave her a crack on her skull.

'See what I mean Joe, she won't hunt,' he said.

The trainer was in no doubt as to just what I thought of him and I was satisfied that at the very least, even if I didn't manage to train her, I had rescued the poor wee mite.

Kit, a cocker spaniel with an induced neurotic aversion to scent.

When I arrived home it was teeming with rain. Despite this, I felt that I just could not put her alone into a strange kennel before I made an effort to befriend her. So I took her into the woods in the hope that she would have a little run about, before I put her away for the night. She didn't run anywhere but just sat there shivering in the cold looking at me, uttering plaintive little whines. It was all I could do to coax her up to me, then I put her inside my jacket for warmth. So, daft as it may appear, we both sat there in the rain with her encased inside my cosy jacket, for quite a long time whilst I comforted her. Eventually I carried her back to the kennels, where I dried and fed her, and left her for the night. On my way over to the house I hoped that she might find that she had discovered a friend.

The next morning I was keen to get her out of kennel as early as possible. Normally, with any new dog at the kennels, for the first few days I would not let them run free until they got to know me for fear of them running away. The treatment for the 'absconding' dog on page 1 will not work in these circumstances for you, the trainer, are a stranger. I knew that this sorrowful wee morsel was going to run nowhere. She crawled behind me, trailing her hind legs, whimpering all the time. There was no doubt that this little dog was going to require big dollops of pleasant stimuli and lots of TLC before there was to be any hope of training her.

I had a piece of ground just off the A74, where I was allowed to train my dogs. It was as the local saying goes, 'fair glazed wi' rabbits'. Now any trainer will tell you, quite rightly, not to let a young dog chase rabbits, especially a cocker, for they can be little devils to steady to the flush of game in their future training. Sound advice; only the breakers would advocate otherwise. (*see* Breakers, page 10)

It was obvious that this little cocker had been well and truly put off hunting. She had been abreacted (conditioned) by associating scent with severe physical chastisement, to the extent that she was now frightened by the merest whiff of scent. I knew then that I had a marathon task on my hands. She was going to need the greatest of encouragement to get her going again – if ever!

The first morning, I climbed over the five-barred gate bordering the lay-by, opposite the Auchencastle hotel on the A74 and carried her well up the hill away from the dual-carriageway. There were rabbits scurrying away in all directions. I put her down and was horrified to note the extent of her neurotic damage. She put up a blood chilling caterwauling. At the first taint of rabbit scent, she lay on her back and wet herself: my initial suspicions were confirmed. She had been battered severely for chasing rabbits. I knew that I had a big problem and what I must do. Come hell or high water I had to get her going again – somehow!

For the next ten days I tried to get her to chase a rabbit of which there were plenty. On the tenth day I saw the first signs of hope. She had been walking by my side, having stopped trailing her legs behind her a few days earlier and was showing less apprehension with my company. Suddenly a rabbit sprang from its seat at our feet and darted off. Kit jumped forward a few paces before coming to a halt and came crawling back to me with her tail between her legs. I gave her a lot of praise. A few paces further up the hill another rabbit obligingly bolted out in front of her and she took off after it. Despite my encouraging calls for her to 'Get On' she stopped once more and slowly started to return to me. This time she winded a rabbit still squatting in its seat, pushed her nose at it and the rabbit broke for freedom. Kit went after it at full tilt to my cries of 'Good Girl – Get On'. The rabbit was lucky, for he made it to the burrow only a split second ahead of her. After a few seconds snuffling at the burrow she headed back to me and again she sighted another rabbit and again was after it to lose it down another burrow. When she returned to me I gave her lots of praise. Don't ever let anyone tell you not to pet a working dog for they can soak up love like a sponge, just like any other dog.

A short time later another rabbit obligingly sprang from its seat in full sight of her and she was immediately in full cry after it. Thirty metres or so on, she stopped for a second and looked back at me. My shouts of 'Good Girl – Good Girl – Get On – Get On!' were sufficient for her to dispel any doubts as to my wishes and she resumed her chase, but by then the rabbit had disappeared. Nevertheless I was pleased to see her get her nose down and follow the line to the burrow. Eventually after another couple of chases she returned to me. Her tail was wagging for the first time, her tongue was lolling, she was breathless and obviously excited, her eyes were glowing like red hot coals and I made a great fuss of her. For all the world her demeanour seemed to be saying, if this is what you want, then I like it.

At last I had cracked it and she would never be 'sticky' again.

By introducing her to the pleasant stimuli of hunting, I had encouraged her to associate hunting with a pleasant, positive and happy experience, as opposed to her previous negative, traumatic and unhappy association. I subsequently trained 'Kit' very successfully and sold her to a client whom I knew to be a gentle man. She lived out the rest of her life happily working for him. I gave her 'trainer' his one hundred pounds and I hope he reads this book.

Advice

This curative regime can be applied to any dog that in your judgement you consider to be 'sticky' in relation to hunting. Through the years I have had to implement this treatment all too frequently, for one reason or another.

Reluctance to hunt can have many causes, not necessarily cruelty. For example, a dog suffering from kennel sickness will tend to be sticky. Anxiety may be the root cause. Inexperience is a possibility. On the other hand, a dog that has been severely chastised, such as 'Kit' may lose confidence and refuse to hunt. Far more frequently however the cause is over training.

In deciding to implement a course of 'free hunting' as your chosen treatment, it is imperative that you assess the individual dog's temperament accurately, before initiating this programme. You must not lose sight of the fact that you will eventually have to reinstate discipline and stop him chasing, when later in his training you reintroduce him to the game, once this remedial course of action is completed. It is of the utmost importance that your assessment of the dog's nature is correct, for if you have diagnosed the fault inaccurately, you will most likely live to regret it.

If you feel that the dog is normally a rather tough exuberant character, although it must be said that it would be most unusual for such a dog to be reluctant to hunt, then proceed with utmost caution. To get a dog like this all steamed up and raring to hunt may be much easier than getting him steady to game once more. Therefore, the moment that you see that he is hunting again and has his tail up and wagging, that's it! No more free hunting.

If on the other hand, you have a sensitive dog, and it is with this type of character where it is much more likely to find the 'sticky' hunter, you can relax and allow a bit more leeway, for, the sensitive dog is always more malleable. Generally, I have found that they tend to be a Prima Donna, more sensitive and intelligent than many of their more robust and boisterous brethren.

No!

Teach this command at every appropriate opportunity, from the very beginning.

Chapter Fifteen

O

Out-Cross Breeding

With little thought being given these days to in-breeding, line breeding or out-cross breeding and more attention being paid to the potential saleability of pups, the pedigrees tend to illustrate a hit or a miss affair. As I have said, it is essential then for the breeder to be able to 'read' the pedigree. If it is your opinion that the first three generations are displaying too much in-breeding, then you would look for a mate that is a complete out-cross to your dog. With the dog that has too much in-breeding, the effect of the familial homozygous genetic characteristics will tend to be over-emphasised, that is for both desired and undesirable traits. In selecting an out-cross for a mating, it must be realised that the aim is to fragment the genetic inheritance in an effort to perhaps breed out the faults that too much in-breeding had brought about. This is, of course, a mating of pure chance and bearing in mind that it is the parents of the sire and dam that contribute to the genetic inheritance, it will be most likely that the entire effect of the out-cross mating will not be fully appreciated until there is the result of a mating from the second generation pups. As it is most desirable to start producing a blood line, the breeder must pin his or her heart on their sleeve and from the results of the out-cross pups, return to a sensible cohesive blood line breeding policy.

(*see* In-Breeding, page 74; Inheritance, page 77; Line Breeding, page 90)

Over! (Intermediate Training)

As soon as possible in the puppy's early days, he should learn the command 'Over', or in the case of a young dog bought at a later age as soon as possible. This should be initiated as part of his daily education. If a pup of perhaps three months old is taught this command, as with the 'Hup' command, it will become so familiar that he will obey it unquestioningly.

If in the course of his daily exercise a wire fence, a gate or some other obstruction should present itself, providing that there is a simple way under, the trainer should climb over, at the same time saying to the pup, 'Over – Good Boy – Over'. Obviously a pup is not going to sprout wings and come sailing over the obstruction, but he will work his way through or under. That is all that is required at this point. We are preparing the way for what is to come in the future, by associating the sound 'Over' with his overcoming the obstacle. It is also desirable to lay the foundations for independence. Consequently providing there is a way through or under, once you have surmounted the obstacle, walk on slowly encouraging him through, but do not help him physically. He must learn this one for himself.

Once again different puppies react in widely different ways. Don't be alarmed by the cacophony and wailing that may go on, just keep slowly increasing the distance, encouraging him all the time vocally. It must be realised that a puppy's eyesight has not fully developed, and some puppies have difficulty in focusing on distant objects, so make allowances. The trainer may get as far away as ten metres or so and the pup get into a real panic. This is unnecessary and it must not be prolonged: the trainer should walk quickly back towards the pup, calling him by name and waving an arm to assist the pup on refocusing and then start again.

I suspect that his eyesight is the least developed sense that the dog possesses, his nose and ears being much more developed and therefore more important. However, as with many other canine attributes this varies greatly from dog to dog.

This exercise in the command 'Over' is, as with many early training activities, merely the forerunner to the more advanced training that is yet to come. I have never experienced any problems in training a dog to jump, if 'training' is the right word, for I have never bothered about specifically constructing 'jumps' as such, relying on the natural obstacles that abounded in the kennel area, such as gates and drystone walls. The method is simple, when the dog is physically capable, I would just climb the wall or obstacle in the normal course of events, leaving the dog to scramble over as best he could. They learned eventually.

However, once the young dog had proved proficient in surmounting obstacles of any kind, I would insist that the dog upon approaching an obstacle should 'Hup' automatically and remain so until ordered 'Over'. This allows the trainer a measure of control whilst negotiating the obstacle himself, but it also prevents the danger of a dog unbidden, jumping over obstacles into possible danger. Once the handler is safely on the other side, he may then call the dog over. Once over, the dog would be 'Hupped' until such times as the trainer orders him to proceed. Never at any time allow a dog to jump barbed wire for such fences can inflict the most horrendous of injuries.

(*see* Creative Imagination, page 22)

Chapter Sixteen

P

Pickled Piper

Away back in the early seventies, I recall an old friend of mine, long dead now, one with an enviable reputation in trials, recounting to me the most frustrating dog in his field trial career. The dog's name? Well, let's call him 'Piper', with whom my friend had a love-hate relationship. He was at his wits' end, for the dog hunted like fury and was a game finder par excellence. Whilst he could contain him on a normal shooting day, but only just, on the trial day the dog was impossible for he seemed to go absolutely ballistic, completely deaf to whistles and blind to hand signals.

There are dogs of a high intelligence, who after being entered into a few trials, seem to realise that this is a special day, and that for some reason, the 'master' appears to let him get away with crimes that would normally incur zero tolerance. This condition is known as 'trial-minded'. Once the trainer recognises this, there is no point in continuing in trials with that particular dog.

If my friend's dog had drawn a high number, then he would hot up all morning and nine times out of ten would be disqualified in his first run. On the other hand, if he had a low number, he would get through his first run and very often with a very good performance, all to be undone, for by the time his turn came in the afternoon, he was so hot that he blotted his copybook once more.

My friend was at the end of his tether and, feeling sorry for him, in hindsight most reprehensible of me but with every good intention, I offered him a possible solution. I had in my possession three phenobarbitone tablets, the remains of a supply the vet had given me for a dog, a long time before, which had turned out to be suffering from epilepsy. I suggested to my friend that perhaps if he were to give the dog one of these, at eight o'clock on the morning of the trial, it would be sufficient to damp down his high spirits a wee bit, and render the dog more amenable to instructions. So on the morning of the trial he gave one to the dog at eight a.m.

On the morning of the trial I asked him quietly if he had taken my advice, to which he nodded. I watched intently his first run, and I had never seen the dog more at one with his handler. Great stuff, I thought, the pill is working. If he keeps this up I'm sure he'll be in with a good chance of at least a place.

At that point a bird was shot to the other dog at the top of the line. 'Piper' drew up smartly to the shot and was sitting in the bracken, quite calmly watching the proceedings. My friend and the judge were watching the other dog's performance too. Eventually the other dog having failed on the bird, the judge asked him if he would like to try for the bird, which he agreed to, for he was not going to pass up the chance of an eye wipe. Turning towards his dog I noted but could not hear that the two men were deep in conversation whilst they walked forward. It was then that I realised that there was no sign of 'Piper'. He appeared to have vanished into thin air. Both men walked forward to investigate, only to find the dog curled up in the bracken snoring his head off. Leaving the line my friend, scowling, muttered to me as he passed carrying the dog, 'You and your damned pills, I've never been so "black-affronted"* in my life.'

I must confess that I avoided his company for the rest of the trial, and the worst thing happened as far as I was concerned – I won it. The following day, anxious about the dog and puzzled at the effect of the pill, I called my friend. When I asked him if the dog was alright, he replied, 'Oh! he's alright, he just woke up about an hour ago'. When I explained my puzzlement regarding the effect that the pill had wreaked upon the dog, he replied, rather sheepishly, 'Well, I've got to confess, I gave him the pill at eight o'clock as you suggested, but when I got to the trial he came bouncing out of the box as bright as a button and I thought, "You bugger, you're as bad as ever, the pill isn't working," I decided that after all, he is a big dog and that pill was awful small, so just to be on the safe side, I gave him the other two.' There's just got to be a moral in there somewhere.

An alternative method of preparing your dog for an impending field trial, apart from working the dog on your own, can be implemented by working with a group of field trial friends. It is really mandatory for these proceedings to be embarked upon by field trial competitors rather than a rough shooting group, simply because the former will be aware of what is required and in their own interests be compliant with the requirements. The rough shooters will not be aware of what is required and do more damage to your dog than good.

Simply put, you will, in the company of your field trial friends, conduct the day's shooting as though you were competing in a field trial. As within the field trial, two dogs will be hunted, but on the sound of a shot they must drop. After a suitable interval, a dog will be sent for the retrieve, but it will never be the dog that flushed the game, he has to sit and watch the other dog bringing in the goods. This is a common incident in a field trial, so what you are doing is manufacturing a situation whereby your dog must curb his jealousy.

* Black Affronted = Embarrassed

Prankish Gun

This was the way that I always prepared my dogs for trials. I would regularly shoot with friends in the 'field trial format'. One day at a trial, upon being summoned into the line, I discovered that my left-hand gun was Dick Laird, Tom's brother.

Before I had time to greet him, he addressed me, 'Are you the Massacre man?' he enquired.

Realising immediately that this was a 'wind up', for Dick, like his brother Tom, had a wicked sense of humour, I replied, 'No – I don't massacre them, I'm the Macsiccar man, it means "make sure".'

'Make sure,' he snorted, and turning to my judge he said, 'You won't be wasting much time with this one, his dogs are rubbish.'

To which the young inexperienced judge replied falteringly, 'Now! now! er, you're not supposed to speak to the handlers.'

'Don't let that worry you,' I interrupted, 'I wouldn't presume to argue on rubbish with him; he's an expert with a lifetime's experience with the "Criffel" dogs.'

In mock anger, Dick replied, 'Oh, I see that's the way of it then. Well, everything you get today will be a runner.'

The judge was becoming frantic by this, 'Every dog has to have an equal chance,' he said.

What the judge did not know was that the dog I had in front of me was unerring on a runner, which Dick knew very well.

After a very successful run I returned to the spectators to be greeted by Tom, 'What was all that about?' he enquired.

When I told him he was less than pleased, 'That's cheating,' he said.

Well I didn't win, so I don't think any damage was done.

Predators

I feel at this late stage of my life, that it is my duty at least, to highlight from experience, some of the tricks that can be employed to dupe the novice trainer. Hopefully my reader will be forewarned and forearmed.

An unscrupulous trainer can 'condition' his dogs in a singularly curious and perverse manner with the express purpose of deceiving the unwary client. Each time he takes a dog out he will follow exactly the same procedure.

Once the minimal hand training is completed, each day thereafter, he will quarter the dog over the same ground, then, at the exactly the same spot every day he will drop the dog by whistle, then after a pause, he would 'hunt' him on again. After a suitable interval, he will fire the blank pistol and drop him once again on the spot where the dog is expecting to be dropped. The 'trainer' will then walk over to the same bush in full view of the dog and chuck a dummy or a rabbit into into it. Without exception this routine is carried out whenever the dog is allowed out from its kennel.

When a client arrives to see his dog, or, a customer comes to the kennels in order to purchase a 'trained' dog, the trainer will take them to the bush and toss a dead rabbit into it, saying something like, 'I'll hunt him up to about there' (pointing to the spot where the dog usually gets the signal by shot to stop) 'then I'll try to handle him out to the blind retrieve.' Needless to say this dog's performance impresses the unsuspecting client and – dog sold.

Undoubtedly to the professional eye, such a subterfuge would be quickly spotted, for the dog would show signs of expectancy as it approached each 'drop' zone. The crowning exposé would be the dash without aid out to a distant unmarked retrieve.

An old client once arrived at my door in suburbia, wishing me to train his dog. He realised upon seeing me that this was not possible. Nevertheless, curiosity got the better of me, so I asked to see his dog. It was six months old, and upon seeing his performance I recognised a very promising pup. My erstwhile client a few weeks later, unbeknown to me, then engaged a professional trainer to train it. As the months went on and ever on, the 'reports' were always glowing to say the least. Anyone who has had a dog professionally trained will know that it is anything but cheap. After nine months of training, my old client decided for financial reasons that enough was enough and telephoned the trainer, indicating that he wished to terminate the training and would collect his dog the following weekend. The trainer pleaded against his taking this action, telling him that the dog was a first class trial contender and that the client would be very foolish to pass up the chance, by cutting the dog's training off prematurely! My ex-client relented to this argument and the dog remained with the professional for another three months. He then decided one day, being in the area on business, to call into the kennels to see his dog, for the first time since he had left it there for training – a year ago!

Caught by surprise, this 'professional' trainer had no option but to produce the dog, explaining to the client as he did so that he would not be seeing the dog at his best, 'for, he's been a bit off colour lately'. When the client saw his dog, he could not believe his eyes at its condition and promptly removed the dog from the kennels. It transpired that the dog was vermin-infested, but most damning of all, it had two fractured ribs and a broken femur. Upon the client telephoning the professional with his complaints, he was brushed off with, 'What are you going to do about this unpaid account?' Apparently the client had not paid for the last month's training. Now there's brass neck for you!

Eventually, once his dog was fit enough, my old client brought the dog back to me for assessment. From the normal enthusiastic boisterous pup that I had seen at six months old, the change in the dog was sad to say the least. He obviously had no idea what a whistle signal meant nor hand signals; and he would not hunt. In my opinion, the dog had had, at best, a minimal amount of training.

Advice

Whether you are a client viewing his dog after it has completed its 'training', or a customer looking for a trained dog, insist that the dog is taken to a shooting area for the demonstration. Accept no excuses – all professionals have several shooting areas. Insist on a proper demonstration of the dog's capabilities of at least two hours. Demand that you see the dog in the rabbit pen. Again, all professional trainers have one. Thereafter ask to see him hunting rabbits out in the open. I specify rabbits as opposed to bird as most dogs in possession of all their faculties will not chase a flying bird, but a rabbit is another matter. There are many dogs who behave impeccably in the rabbit pen who can be very wild out of it. As I have said, dogs are not stupid, they know that they can be caught in the pen whereas it's an entirely different game out of it.

Preparation for a Field Trial (Advanced Training)

This may take the form of simply maximising the dog's speed in relation to the length of time that a normal run in a field trial would be. It is really just down to the individual dog handler's common sense. If a dog is expected to work non-stop throughout a normal shooting day, he will pace himself accordingly. Thereby he will not hunt up to his full capacity, consequently, for the handler to take his dog into a trial without properly preparing him for it, there is every probability that his lack of speed will not appeal to the judge.

In my view, due to the contemporary field trial judges' obsession with speed, it is in the competitor's interest if he wishes to succeed in a field trial, to present his dog at its full potential. At this point it might be opportune for me to explode a few fallacies. There are some people who actually believe that a small dog is faster than its larger counterpart. It certainly may appear so, but it merely *appears* to be faster, because it is smaller. It is because of this fallacious view that the breeders are encouraged to breed smaller and smaller spaniels, which does the breed no good. Then there are those who hold to the view that a light-coloured dog is faster than a dark-coloured dog, again, misconstrued generalisation and as such, utter nonsense. The lighter dog merely appears to be faster and it is an optical illusion. Whilst a slow pottering gundog is to be abhorred, there is evidence to suggest that there are instances where a fast and stylish dog can actually outrun his nose! On numerous occasions I have seen a speedy dog actually skid to a halt to turn and work his way back to the find. There are therefore reasonable grounds for assuming that there must be occasions when a dog will outrun his nose, and game go undetected and unnoticed by his handler, especially if the dog's speed is greater than his powers of scent.

Providing the dog handler has confidence in his dog's scenting capabilities, the following routine is recommended in preparing his dog for a trial. The handler will adopt a means whereby he can frustrate the dog as much as possible by hunting him in predetermined intervals of limited time. The procedure is to hunt him for twenty minutes, knowing that it would be very unusual for a dog to be under the judge's scrutiny for a lengthier period of time in the field trial. The dog is then put on the lead and walked for twenty minutes, and it is essential that he is walked for this period of time, so that he is constantly being assailed by scent, so do not be lazy and sit down for a while. During this period it will be noted that the dog will be 'hotting up'. At the end of the lead period, the dog is then hunted again for another twenty minutes, and so on. Hopefully, the result of this treatment will be that your dog will hunt at the top of his capabilities throughout his spells in front of the judges.

The individual dog's temperament will indicate the regime that he will require, for if the dog is normally a rumbustious character, he will probably require no encouragement whatsoever in the speed department. This type of dog, instead of requiring encouragement to 'hot up' before a trial will indicate that they require to be 'cooled down' if success in a trial is to be envisaged. With a dog that tends to hot up excessively at a field trial, the treatment is the opposite to that which would be given to the dog that requires some 'gee-ing up' in preparation for an oncoming trial. Such dogs require to be extensively shot over and worked hard all day, for at least three days prior to the trial. This procedure should be carried on right up to the day before the trial.

Springers cooling off.

Advice

As I have indicated, there are dogs that do not require a series of pepping-up exercises, for they hot up by themselves at the field trial. It may be the crowds, the scent around them, the sound of the guns, or just the entire milieu, but these dogs can be a positive nightmare. Bad enough if you only have one dog with you, but hell on earth if you have two or three entries in the trial. You will not require to be a genius to recognise the dog, for he's the one that you can hardly control on a normal shooting day – the dog that has a mind of his own. As the trial progresses he will become more and more frustrated and excited and will constantly pull on his lead. All professional handlers and many amateur handlers have experienced this phenomenon and there is really very little that can be done about it at the trial. Many handlers will stop at every stream or puddle and, taking a handful of water, wipe the dog's muzzle with it. I must plead guilty to having indulged in this myself, but I suspect that it has little or no effect other than a psychological one on the handler.

Professional Trainers

Allow me to make it quite clear at this point that, in the sixties when I started training professionally there were as far as I am aware, at best only six professional gundog trainers in the UK, that is to say, trainers whose entire livelihood depended solely on the training of gundogs. There were a multitude of amateur trainers who figured conspicuously, indeed were virtually in control of field trials especially in Scotland.

It is in the professional trainer's own interests to offer clients his very best efforts in training their dog, for he is well aware that 'word of mouth' is by far the best advertising. It is by no means unusual to get repeat business from a satisfied customer.

The same applies when he sells a dog for he has to be certain that the dog is a worthy ambassador for his kennels and his expertise as a trainer. Probably the best source for his continued business is from the selling of puppies, for it is from these that in many instances he will get his training contracts. It is also of the greatest importance therefore, that to the eye of his customers the kennels should be clean and the dogs obviously well fed and fit. Very often clients will purchase a puppy over the telephone and request that it should be delivered by rail. It goes without saying that the trainer is aware that the only criteria by which he is judged in such circumstances, are by the appearance and condition in which the buyer finds the pup at the station.

Through the years I have encountered and had dealings with all the professional trainers and I can assure my reader that the dishonest 'fly-by-night' is very much the exception, rather than the rule.

Most sensible trainers try their utmost to be fair with their clients. It is merely the oddities that throw the majority into disrepute.

Professionalism

Perhaps I have been lucky, for in all my years as a professional trainer I only had one client's dog die in my care. He was a yellow Labrador belonging to a doctor who lived in Kent. The dog had finished its training and was ready to be taken home. The doctor had paid six months' fees on the dot every month, a perfect client. Due to the distance involved he had not been able to visit the dog at any time during its training. However I had been able each month to keep him informed of progress, my last report being on the Thursday night, when to his query I was able to assure him that his was an excellent dog and should perform well for him. We arranged for the doctor to collect him on the following Saturday, when I would demonstrate the dog for him.

In those days I had four kennel maids, so imagine my horror on the Friday night when one of my kennel girls reported that 'Sandy has a funny lump on his head'. I rushed over to the kennels suspecting rather unjustly that one of the girls had given him a clout with a broom or something. My heart chilled on what I saw, even in the few minutes since Margaret had reported it to me, she said that the lump had grown significantly. I rushed over to the house and 'phoned for the vet, who said he would come immediately. There was no point however for upon my return to the kennels 'Sandy' was dead. Further investigation revealed that up to three p.m. he had shown no symptoms. The vet diagnosed cancer.

I telephoned my client the doctor, to be told that he was on his way to Scotland. What was I to do? How would it look to the doctor? After six months of glowing reports he was about to arrive at my kennels to be told that his dog had died at the eleventh hour. Even if he believed me, there was always going to be the little nagging doubt as to just what had been going on.

I waited apprehensively for his arrival the next morning, but I knew what I was going to do. He drew up in his car all smiles. 'Jim', I said, 'do you see that springer there?' indicating a liver and white spaniel. 'Well she's a field trial winner, so she's worth a bit of money and I'm showing her to you for sadly you're not going to be able to take "Sandy" home. I'm sorry to say, he died last night, so I am giving this bitch to you.' After his initial shock regarding 'Sandy' he began to protest, saying things like, 'Look Joe, you're not responsible it could have happened to anybody.' I told him that nobody was going to leave my kennels emptyhanded after paying me six months' training fees, for, with the best will in the world, it would look bad for me. Eventually after a demonstration, Jim went home a satisfied client. When the word got out in the Kent shooting circles, I just couldn't count how many dogs I received for training over the next few years. I like to think that I acted in a professional way. One thing is certain, honesty pays.

Chapter Seventeen

Q

Quartering (Intermediate & Advanced Training)

This is an aspect of training that some handlers appear to have difficulty with. There are those who have only experienced success by throwing pieces of biscuit for the dog, first to one side of the dog's quartering beat and then at the other as they walked the ground. I have never subscribed to this school of thought, believing that such practices could lead to a pottering dog.

If possible, find a piece of ground which is fairly open and containing some light ground cover, i.e. sparse rushes, rough grass, heather or bracken. Avoid thick cover such as gorse bushes at this stage, for the handler wants to see his hunting dog at all times. Moreover, the object of this exercise is to teach the dog in a pattern of ground treatment. This will never be achieved in gorse bushes, or any kind of heavy ground cover such as brambles.

Leave the young dog in the car and with an older dog, walk any game off the ground in the manner described in Discouraging Game (page 30), then after returning the old campaigner to the car, take the young dog to the prepared ground, release him and tell him to 'Get On!' In the early days with this exercise, always proceed into a facing wind, so that any scent will waft towards the dog. He should go bounding out to one side or the other. With the whistles that are used for the 'recall' signal, give one short sharp 'peep', call his name and as soon as he glances your way, indicate with your arm the direction that you wish him to take, whilst at the same time altering your own direction and proceeding slowly in the same route. If all goes well the dog should come trotting or running across your path. As soon as he has progressed past you for perhaps three metres, give another short sharp 'peep' on the whistle and, if necessary, call his name if he does not respond, utter the final deterrent, drop him, walk slowly up to him and together with the 'turn' whistle signal, give his ear a tug. Upon returning to his stance, the handler must once again indicate the opposite direction to that in which the dog had been going and walk in that direction also. The dog should once again come bounding past you. As you proceed forwards in this zig-zag fashion it should be relatively simple to control him in a fairly methodical pattern. If this is incorporated in the general format of the everyday routine it will be found that as time goes by, the handler can gradually narrow his zig-zag pattern into a fairly straight line until he is walking slowly forwards (*see* figure, page 116). But, and this is of paramount importance, never, throughout a spaniel's life, fall into the trap of walking forwards at too fast a pace. In other words, give the dog time to work his ground at all times or you will soon destroy any pattern that you have taught him (*see* figure, page 117).

I have found that many 'guns' in a field trial have no dog sense whatsoever and it can be a positive nightmare trying to give the dog a chance to hunt his ground adequately. Surprising though it may seem, I have noticed also, that on far too many occasions, I have been forced to draw the judge's attention to this. The real danger in this situation is that the dog will miss game and some judges might be too quick to disqualify the handler.

Do not blow a whistle just for the sake of it. As time goes on you will find

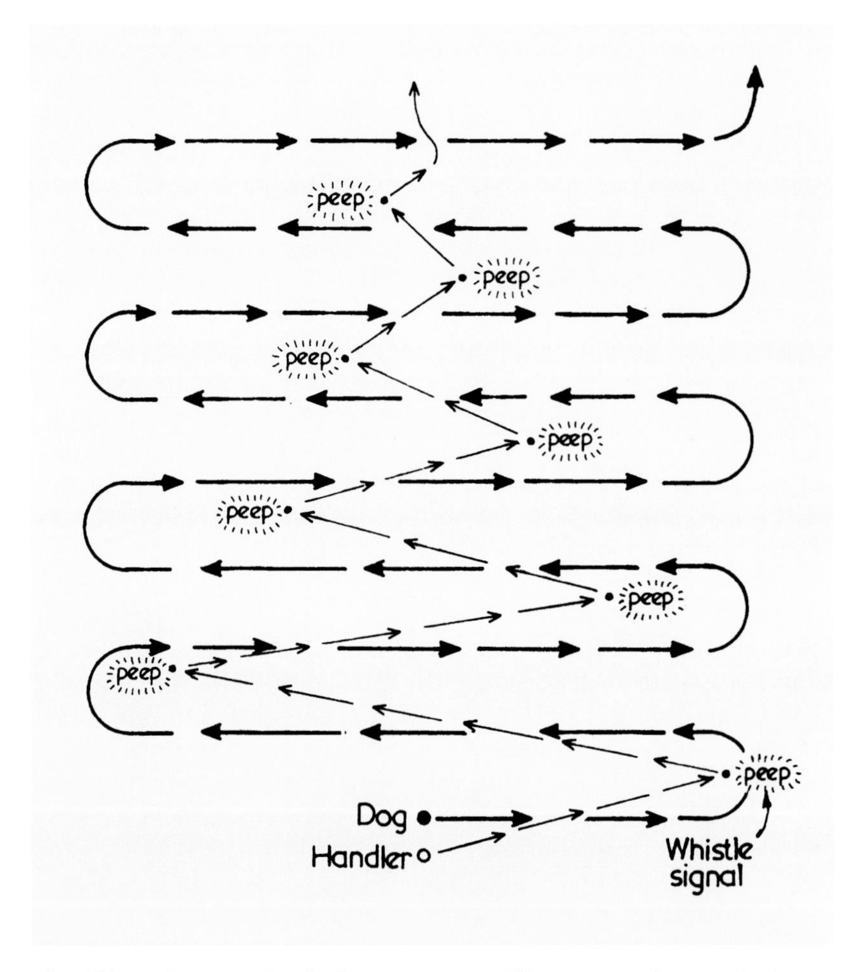

It will be quite some time before you can modify your own 'quartering'.

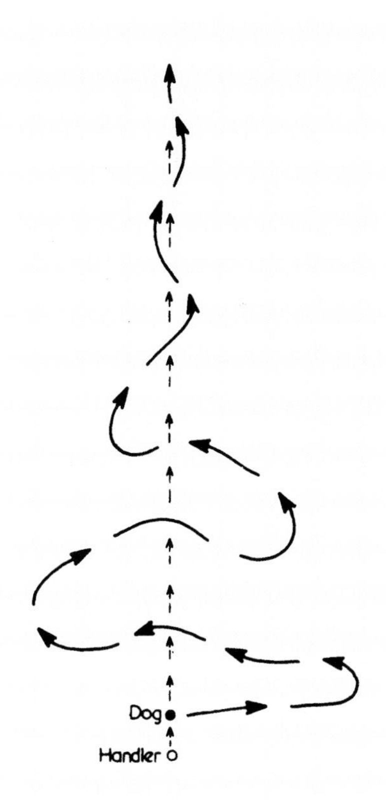

that providing you have been consistent and turned the dog at roughly the same distance from you each time, he will begin to turn by himself, only requiring reminding every now and then. But vigilance is important. If you are inattentive he will quickly realise it and take advantage.

Occasionally you may find that the dog will tend to pull out ahead, probably with his nose down on a foot scent. This is known as 'lining' and the better the dog's nose the more guilty of this he is liable to be. Without stopping his progress, recall him with the two sharp repetitive 'peeps' on the recall whistle, and as he comes back to you swing him off in the direction that you want him to go. You are now well on the way to possessing a dog that will work a methodical pattern with the aid of whistles, within shot at all times.

This is probably the best time to draw my readers' attention to another of those little 'trade secrets'. From the very beginning, even before the dog has become fully conditioned to his 'ground treatment' he must have his hunting area quite severely curtailed. This means merely that you must hold the dog tight in his pattern of ground treatment. In other words, let us visualise what area of ground that ultimately, in the future you would wish the dog to hunt in his ground treatment within shot. You would probably consider that if he were to cover four metres either side of his beat and no farther than four metres in front, you would be well pleased. To have any hope of achieving this ideal, you are required in his early training in ground treatment to hold him to a tight pattern of perhaps two and a half metres either side of you and no more than two and a half metres in front. As far as is possible (for some dogs, depending on their temperament and nose, are much more difficult to 'hold' than others) you will maintain that area of ground treatment throughout his training and first shooting season.

The reason for this is simple. Little difficulty will be experienced in the dog's ground treatment training and perhaps two-thirds of his first shooting season, depending again on the individual dog's intelligence, temperament, nose etc.; but from then on, as his growing experience allows him to realise his role in this world and as he progresses, he will begin to recognise the different scents and the creatures that these emanate from. Thereafter, he will become much more involved in his hunting and gradually as he gets keener, bit by bit, he will take up ground and the trainer will allow him to do this. In this way the dog eventually works his ground within the 'box' approximately four by four metres, either side of his handler and four metres in front. The trainer who is not aware of this and allows his dog too much ground to hunt during the training in ground treatment, is the handler who ends up with a dog hunting barely within shot.

As the dog 'quarters' the ground it is a good idea if, every now and again, the handler catches the dog's eye, raises his hand and calls the dog to 'Hup'. The chances are that the dog will drop and when he does this will allow the trainer to walk slowly up to him and praise him. This must not be done too often however, for if it is, the dog will start to anticipate the command to the detriment of his concentration and thereby become 'sticky' and unsure.

There are trainers who place their faith in the check cord to teach ground treatment to their dogs. The idea being that whilst the dog is running about, a short sharp 'peep' is given with the plastic pea-less whistle accompanied by a tug on the cord to turn him. My argument regarding the use of a check cord in teaching the dog to quarter his ground is exactly the same as my contention to using this contrivance in the rabbit pen. To these trainers I can only say, credit your dog with the intelligence to know when he is tethered to a cord and when he is not.

There are a few problems that may arise in 'teaching' a dog to quarter his ground. A sensitive dog is inclined, when any new exercises are first introduced, to feel insecure and to display this insecurity in many ways. With this type of pupil, after he has been turned at the periphery of his beat a few times with the whistle, he may slow his pace and look warily at his handler; he may even stop moving altogether and just stand there with his tail between his legs. Neither is it at all unusual for the dog to manifest his unhappiness with this new lesson by returning and sitting in front of the handler. The answer to all signs of insecurity is reassurance. To encourage him, stroke and speak to him in a soothing happy tone. Normally, he will work his way

Springer on the alert.

through his initial fears, for these are pure and simply a lack of confidence. Nevertheless, the handler is walking on eggs, so if after a few days the dog does not appear to be progressing, relax the quartering exercises and return to them after a week or so.

Do not indulge in any kind of training, except water work, during a heat wave. The only time suitable for training during such conditions is in the early morning or in the evening.

If in the early stages of quartering exercise the dog is hunted into the wind (upwind beat), the dog should naturally turn at the end of his beat, into the wind. If not, he may develop into a downwind turner, which any competent trial judge would spot immediately and mark the dog down. Therefore, downwind turning is extremely undesirable if the dog is intended for competing in field trials, although it may not be thought to be such a problem in the normal shooting day situation. It has to be said though, that if the handler persists in the dog's early quartering in hunting him on a 'down wind' (following wind), this will encourage the dog to develop into a downwind turner. The handler in the dog's early ground treatment should as much as possible, always hunt him into the wind.

Some trainers like to use a ploughed field for quartering sessions. Crossing the field with the furrows running from left to right, the dog will tend to utilise the bottoms of the furrows to run on.

Quartering – Cheek Wind Beat (Intermediate & Advanced Training)

Clear the ground of any game as described on page 30. As with any form of ground treatment, this cannot be taught. It is purely dependent on the dog's scenting capabilities, together with some guidance from the handler in keeping the dog within shot. As time goes by, the dog's growing experience and scenting powers will assist him to adapt accordingly.

Upon telling the dog to 'Get On', the handler will allow the dog to take up ground, and if the wind is coming from the left, the handler will cast the dog straight out on his right side, similar to that described in the down wind beat. Once the handler considers the dog to be at a comfortable distance, approximately four to five metres, he will turn him with the short sharp 'peep' of the plastic pea-less whistle in conjunction with the appropriate hand signal, partially crouching down and making the imaginary 'patting' motion to encourage the dog to come back. In making his turn, the dog will be facing into the wind with its myriad of scents thereby bringing his scenting powers into play. This procedure is repeated. (*see* figure, page 125) A dog, depending on his scenting capabilities, will soon adapt to this naturally. If the wind direction is from the right, then the dog's initial cast will be from the left. It is important for the trainer to realise that it is necessary to stand still until the dog has had time to work all of his ground across its beat from right to left or vice versa, depending on the wind direction, and up to the trainer's feet before moving on, as outlined in *Quartering – Down Wind Beat* page 123. The handler will then be able take up his new position forwards level with where the dog had initially turned farthest away from him and the dog will then continue with his ground treatment by hunting a fresh beat.

If a trainer gets the opportunity to compare several dogs' reaction in respect of wind treatment, as with any other aspect relating to their environment, they will react in a wide variety of ways. Naturally, in the ground treatment in relation to the prevailing wind direction and scenting conditions, the better the nose the more marked the dog's reactions and resultant performance will be. If he has a good nose, obviously he will be acutely sensitive to every idiosyncrasy of air current and scent. On the other hand, a dog with poor scenting capabilities will show little or no reaction to variance in scenting conditions. It is this dog that, in all probability, will prove to be the biggest headache for the trainer when involved in the downwind or cheek wind beat. There is little that can be done in such a situation; either the dog should be sent back to its owner or, as is by no means unusual, the trainer is asked to do the best he can.

On an upwind beat a dog's capabilities in the scenting department or lack of, whatever the case may be, make themselves apparent in several different

Ground scent.

Air scent.

ways. Generally speaking, the gifted dog with an acute sense of smell will display a much more irregular pattern as he quarters his ground. He will invariably turn into the wind at the end of each cast; furthermore, he will break off at intervals, slow down momentarily and 'feather' from side to side as he investigates every little pocket of scent with his nose close to the ground, and then speeding up again, proceeds on his way to complete his beat. At intervals he may slow his pace, head up, with a slight prancing gait from side to side as he catches airborne body scent. In the majority of cases there appears to be quite a decisive link between a dog's scenting talents and body language, for very often a dog well-endowed with scenting aptitudes is far more stylish than his less endowed counterpart, all of which tend to make such a dog exciting and aesthetically pleasing to the eye. A dog that possesses 'no nose', on the other hand, performs at a uniform speed at all times and as a result is about as exciting as watching paint dry. Scenting conditions, whether good, bad or patchy, are not going to play much of an influential part in his ground treatment. Upwind, downwind, cheek wind, good scent or bad will not influence his speed, style – if any – nor pattern; almost invariably his pattern of ground treatment resembles that of car windscreen wipers.

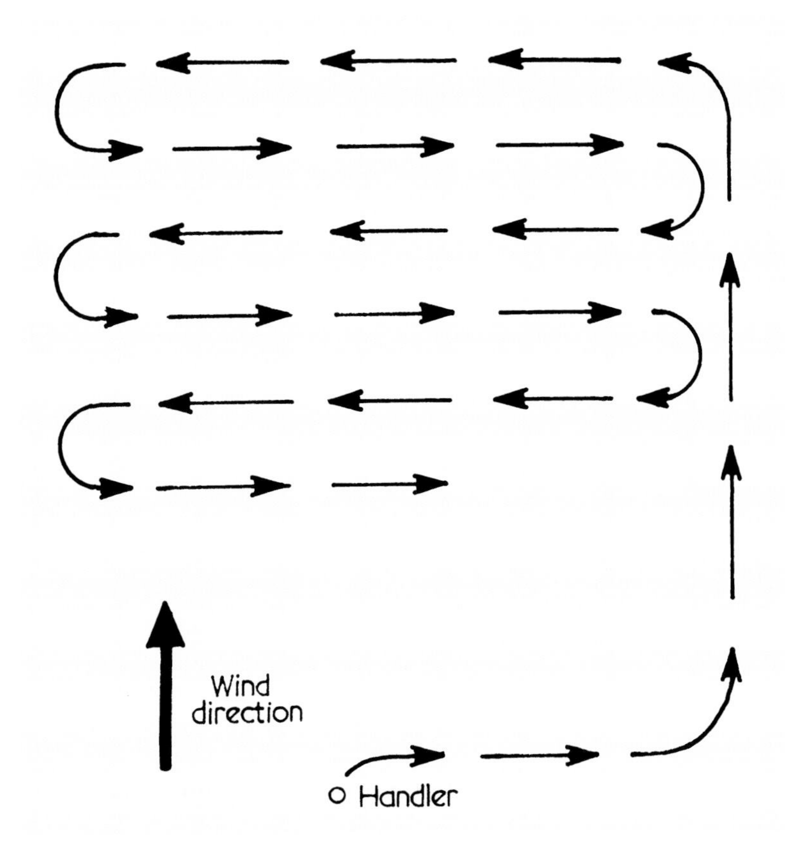

This exercise demands all your attention; do not be lax – work him – insist that he turns on the 'turn whistle'.

Quartering – Down Wind Beat (Advanced Training)

Again as outlined on page 30, make sure that the ground has been cleared of game.

Ground treatment is perhaps the only area where the trainer can be sure that practice makes perfect, for there is little chance of the dog becoming bored by it. It is always a good plan though, to exercise a little caution and therefore indulge in it initially in small doses. Remember that the longer the dog is out with his trainer, the more likely the chances are of running into a problem and it is imperative that, especially in the early stages of any 'new' approach, we dwell on success.

It is for this reason that until the dog has demonstrated that he is proficient in his ground treatment when hunting into the wind – that it has become an ingrained good habit – the trainer should not progress further in his ground treatment regarding the cheek or upwind aspect of his education. The trainer must be one hundred per cent satisfied with the dog's progress, for it is very tempting on approaching the chosen venue and finding the wind in the wrong direction to be lazy and, rather than walking the dog on the lead until you have the wind direction in your favour before releasing him, to 'make do' and hunt him with the wind in the wrong direction for your purposes.

This is just another small, but all important point. If you do not pay special heed to it you are most unlikely ever to get a tight pattern into the dog, for working a dog down the wind naturally encourages him to pull out down the wind and in the early stages of ground treatment this is most undesirable. I have included all aspects of ground treatment in relation to the wind direction within this chapter, for it is desirable that all are 'taught' in the intermediate and advanced stages of the dog's education. Once the dog is proficient in his ground treatment in relation to all wind directions, it is very important that for the rest of the dog's training and right up to the end of the dog's first shooting season, the dog should be hunted into the wind whenever possible.

Before commencing with the down wind beat exercise, as always, ensure that the training ground has been cleared of game before taking the young dog on to it. On arrival take off his lead and immediately command him to 'Hup!' endorsed with the hand signal. You may think it is unnecessary in such a situation – it is not – for you are showing the dog that it is you who are in control. If the trainer is inconsistent and does not progressively instil good habits in the dog by repetitive actions, he should not be surprised if he encounters an inconsistent performance from his dog later on. Although this may seem pedantic, it is very important. Put the lead slowly and deliberately into your pocket whilst keeping an eye on him, and any signs of fidgeting or impatience on his part, such as squeaking, should be discouraged by a stern 'No!'

Here I must tell you that there are many young dogs even into the teens of months old that will utter a 'squeak' through frustration or excitement upon first being cast off. Whist this is most undesirable, I would not be too concerned about it at this early stage, for very often this is just the exuberance of youth and diminishes with maturity. Most assuredly, you do not want a 'musical' dog out shooting with you and in the field trial scene it is virtually the kiss of death for this merits immediate disqualification.

My contention is as I have said on page 170 regarding 'Yipping', it is one thing for a dog to give full-blooded 'voice' whilst shooting or in a field trial, where merciless severe judgement is undoubtedly justifiable. It is quite another matter though, to penalise a dog for the merest squeak of excitement, especially if in the same trial a noisy handler is heard 'giving tongue' of many more decibels than any squeaking dog is capable of, yet goes unpunished.

I believe implicitly that if the dog has reached a high standard of efficiency in his ground treatment under conventional conditions, i.e. the upwind beat, he will adapt quite readily, requiring little assistance from the trainer once he is faced with the downwind beat.

When a dog finds game he is invariably downwind of it. The trainer will

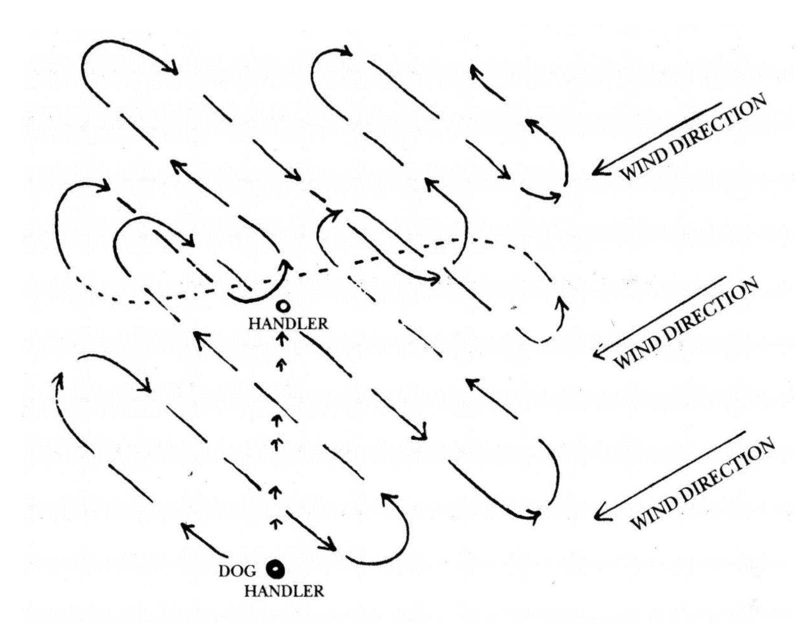

The cheek wind treatment
The dog is cast off 'downwind', turned into the wind and allowed time to work the ground in front of the handler. Once he has satisfactorily covered his ground and is then 'upwind', his handler may then proceed forward, ready to commence the next beat.

realise then, that to work a beat with the wind in his rear, he must be sent down the wind, turned with the single 'peep' of the plastic pea-less whistle and allowed to work the ground back to the trainer's feet so that he is facing into the wind. To allow him to do this to the best advantage you, the trainer, must stand still. (*see* Quartering – Cheek Wind Beat, page 120) Obviously if this small but important point is ignored, as it very often is and consequently the trainer moves forward whilst the dog is still working the ground back to him, he will be taking up spare, possibly game-holding ground that the dog has not had the opportunity to hunt. It follows then that tightly 'tucked in' game will be missed by the dog, for there are few dogs that will hunt ground that has already been passed over by his handler.

Again I must point out that this is another situation that can prove problematical for the handler in a field trial, for it is up to the handler to control his dog, and thereby, if necessary ask the judge to keep the 'guns' in check, so that the dog is given a chance to hunt all of his ground thoroughly. The handler should not feel intimidated by this, for he is entitled to ask and cannot be penalised for doing so.

Whether in a field trial or the shooting field, a trainer who neglects to allow the dog to work all of his ground thoroughly by 'poaching' some of the dog's ground, and does this as a habit, will find that the dog will soon anticipate this and, as a result, will only make a token gesture regarding the intervening ground, resulting in his forming the habit of pulling out to extreme shotgun range, turning into the wind at intervals to quest a likely piece of cover, then proceeding once more to 'pull out' until he is hunting out of shot. Never forget that one problem tends to beg another; it does not take much foresight to realise that this is the embryonic stage of the 'wild' dog that hunts out of shot at all times, no matter what wind direction or scenting conditions are (*see* figure, page 117).

After casting the dog off with the usual verbal 'Get On!', the trainer will remain on the spot and by turning the dog at approximately five metres, he will 'work' his dog back to his feet. As in the other aspects of ground treatment, the handler will notice that after he has turned the dog, providing it has a serviceable nose at all, that to a greater or lesser degree the dog will commence 'quartering' his ground back to him naturally. It is, once again, this basic instinct that the trainer takes advantage of and embellishes to his own ends, occasionally indicating with a single 'peep' on the plastic pea-less whistle and an indicative hand signal when he thinks it appropriate to direct the dog in the direction in which he wishes his dog to go.

Should the dog tend to hunt spasmodically and perhaps dwell overlong on one spot, clicking your tongue will help to 'gee' him up, or, tell him to 'leave it'. On the other hand, should he show a tendency to turn back to you, hunt a small patch, then turn once more down the wind away from you, perhaps on some foot scent or other, stop him with the 'thunderer' stop whistle. Then call him back to you with the two rapid 'peep-peeps' with the plastic pea-less return whistle combined with the hand-patting signal and, as he makes his way back to you, using the single 'peep' from the same whistle, you may then swing him off to either side of his beat.

It is worth noting that whilst a dog is head down and moving, in many instances he will be 'whistle deaf' to the 'turn' or 'return' whistle signal. It is therefore much easier to exercise the final deterrent, the 'thunderer' stop whistle. If properly trained, it would be an exceptional dog indeed that did not drop to it, for the sound is quite distinct from any other whistle. Once dropped, the dog's whole attention will be devoted to the handler and therefore the dog will be much more compliant to obeying the next command.

The average dog 'cottons on' to just what is required of him regarding the downwind beat. However, that is no excuse for being careless – always work the dog and keep a watchful eye on him; what today appears as just a small instance of naughtiness is tomorrow's problem; dogs are past masters at driving in, little by little, the thin edge of the wedge.

Chapter Eighteen

R

Rabbit Pen Construction

A rabbit pen, its construction, maintenance and last, but by no means least, its inhabitants, measure up to a not inconsiderable expense and amount of work for the gundog trainer. To the reader who may wish to build a rabbit pen, I have to say that it can be a very expensive luxury. I say luxury, for in my view there is really no need for the amateur to go to the expense. However, if my reader is determined, then allow me to provide a cheap method.

Most gundog books stipulate that the most important criterion in building a pen is that it must be escape-proof. The readers are then advised to dig a trench one metre deep around the perimeter, within which corrugated galvanised iron sheets are placed to prevent escape by burrowing. In my view a pen of less than quarter of an acre is of little use whatsoever. The reader will then appreciate that a trench dug as described around such an area is no small task and rather expensive.

The cheapest alternative is to fence off an area of perhaps one acre. Along the bottom of the fence, a one-metre width of chicken wire is laid flat on the ground and joined with wire clips at five centimetre intervals to the vertical wire fence, which can be as high as you like. Until the grass grows through and thereby anchors it, a good plan is to lay stones at intervals to keep the netting flat on the ground. Another length of one metre wide wire is attached by wire clips at intervals to inward-sloping pieces of wood around the top of the fence. As a precaution against fox raids, three strands of pulsating electric twelve volt strands of plastic cord through which thin wire is strung should be attached to outward-sloping pieces of timber at the top.

Within the the pen, various areas of cover should be arranged. If for instance, heaps of tree branches are provided these will quickly form good areas of cover as the grass grows up within them. Small bushes, depending on the size of the pen, can be planted which, in time, will also afford some shade as well as concealment for the rabbit. Lengths of drainage pipes scattered around will also allow the rabbits shelter and refuge from the dogs. Protection from weasels and stoats is also to be recommended, so fen traps at intervals within tunnels around the edge of the pen will minimise rabbit casualties.

Some authorities recommend the use of tame rabbits to 'stock' the pen. I have to say that I have never found this method successful, for the tame rabbit appears to be reluctant to bolt and when he does, it is more of a hop, skip and a jump, stopping just a few yards away, usually in full view of the pup. All very frustrating for both the pup and his trainer. Through the years I have also noted a very marked difference in the dogs' behaviour between working up to a tame and the wild rabbit. I can only conclude then, that there is a different scent to the tame rabbit as opposed to the wild.

Without doubt the wild rabbit is by far the best proposition. These are easily procured with the aid of 'muzzled' ferrets and a few purse nets. As they bolt, put them into a sack; they will stay there immobile provided you keep the sack beside you. However at the first sign that the rabbits cannot hear you, they will slice through the sack like a hot knife through butter, to be off in a flash. It is illegal to transport live wild rabbits.

In the sixties and seventies whilst the devastating effects of myxomatosis were affecting most of the country (it first appeared on a farm in Dumfries, in September 1954), it was a necessity for the professional as well as the amateur trainers who trained in a semi-professional capacity (that is, with more than just a few dogs) to have access to a rabbit pen. Indeed in England, up to the late seventies and in some areas even into the early eighties, the rabbit was very scarce indeed or even non-existent. It was not unusual in those times for little groups of field trial enthusiasts to rent rabbit shooting in Scotland for perhaps a week or more, in preparation for the Scottish trials, which in many instances were held almost exclusively on ground thickly populated with rabbits.

The rabbit having made a remarkable comeback during the late eighties and nineties, there seems little need for the amateur trainer to build a rabbit pen these days. This may not be entirely accurate however, for I am aware that even today there are little groups of field trial enthusiasts who still book a week or so rabbit shooting in this area, in order to prepare their dogs for the trial season.

Nevertheless, as far as the rabbit pen is concerned, I have known spaniels who were almost ruined by being over-used in the pen. The pen is only of value in teaching the novice dog steadiness to the flush of the rabbit and the stop whistle. It will not improve the dog's game finding ability, nor as I have been informed some seem to believe, will its use help the dog improve his scenting capabilities. The ground in any rabbit pen is polluted by pungent rabbit scent, so much so that far from helping the dog it is more likely to confuse him. Dogs are not stupid. As with knowing that they cannot misbehave on a 'check cord' or electric collar, they are also equally aware that such is not the case when they are running free. Similarly, overuse in the pen will only demonstrate to them that there is every likelihood that the handler will catch them in the close confines of the pen. Once out of the pen I have known

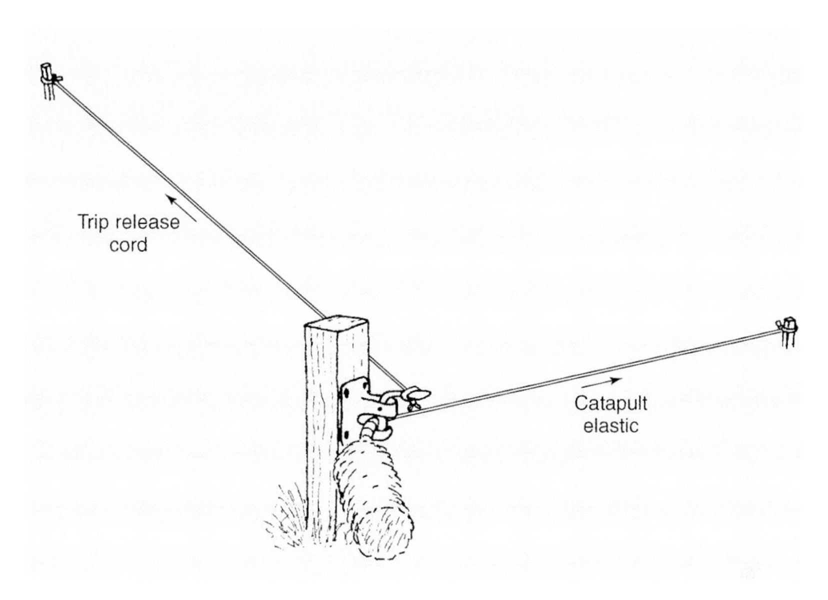

Simulated 'bolting rabbit' trip release.

dogs that were as wild as a hawk. The rabbit pen then is only of use whilst the pup is still unaware of what is required of him regarding steadiness to ground game. Once he has been taught that lesson, then my advice is most definitely, no more rabbit pen unless there is a breakdown in his steadiness to ground game in his later training, in which case a refresher course in the pen would be advisable.

Apart from the full-time professional trainer, who has many dogs to put before the rabbit and is required to demonstrate the steadiness of a dog to clients at a moment's notice, in these times of little difficulty in procuring rabbity ground, I can see no justification for the amateur trainer to go to the expense and get involved in the labour required to build a rabbit pen. There are alternatives.

Rabbit Pen Substitutes

It may be that in the one-man-one-dog situation, the trainer does not have access to 'gamey' ground. There is no need to despair about this, for by using initiative and ingenuity there is much that can be done to alleviate this problem, although unfortunately it entails a little extra work.

A 'bolting' rabbit can be quite easily simulated by using a length of catapult elastic approximately five metres long, a gate-latch and a post. Attach one end of the elastic to a peg hammered into the ground and the other end to a rabbit skin dummy, preferably with a freshly cured rabbit skin on it. The elastic is then stretched to its full capacity and clicked into a gate-latch which has been attached to another post hammered into the ground. A 'release' cord is then attached to the gate-latch and at a suitable distance pegged into the ground. (*see* figure, page 129) It helps to encourage the dog if a trail is laid using a cold rabbit, criss-crossed over the area which is to be hunted by him. Three or four of these devices scattered over a sizeable area of ground, whilst they are no substitute for the real thing, will go a long way to steadying a young dog.

The dummy launcher can also be utilised for steadying purposes, by launching a rabbit-skin dummy ahead of him, low along the ground, whilst the dog is hunting. Upon his hearing the report, the dog will drop to the 'shot' and see the tumbling dummy, which bears a striking resemblance to the toppled rabbit in the shooting situation. This is an extremely dangerous weapon and care must be taken to prevent the dog being struck by the propelled dummy, for serious injury could ensue.

Pigeon release cages are now available from the gundog training manufacturers. By camouflaging these in cover, these can simulate a flushed bird very realistically, thereby rendering obsolete the need to 'dizzy pigeon' as described in *Training Spaniels*.

(*see* Stinking Out page 146)

Retrieves – Frozen (Intermediate & Advanced Training)

The following is classed as advanced training and is certainly more interesting for the trainer. It is obviously very tempting for the amateur trainer to start the advanced retrieving too soon, but if you are too impatient and rush any aspect of training then you will pay the price, so – slowly does it.

One lucky day in Carlisle, enquiring in a local shop as to what was their largest freezer for sale, the salesman pointed out to me in his window, a specially made freezer of thirty-two cubic feet, which, he said had been manufactured for display only and had been on show for some considerable time and consequently had suffered some wear and tear. As a result I got it at a bargain price. Because of its size, I stationed it in one of my numerous outhouses at the kennels. From then on, I had an inexhaustible supply of 'cold' game on hand throughout the year for retrieving purposes. I hasten to add that all game which was intended for the dogs' retrieving purposes was carefully labelled, so that it would not be confused with game which was intended for the family table!

Frozen game must not be confused with 'cold' game, that is, game that the trainer had shot the previous day, and left overnight for rigor mortis to have set in and taken effect, stiffening the corpse. In presenting the 'retrieve' in this way, the dog, who until now has only carried dummies, which tend to be solid and unyielding, in picking up the stiff rabbit, is progressing through his training in a seemingly natural transition.

Nor should my reader be confused as to which is preferred by the professional trainer, cold or frozen, thawed-out game. There is no contest. In all training, the most natural method is always preferred, therefore, in this case, it is the cold game that would be the choice. If the professional trainer could guarantee sufficient game supplies so that he could provide for his numerous pupils a steady supply of cold game, then obviously he would. However, in the professional kennel environment, such a steady supply of game would be impracticable, because of the limited shooting season. It would also require the trainer to be shooting rabbits every day and he just does not have the time to spare for that.

Pheasant, rabbit, pigeon, teal, widgeon and lastly taking into account the slightly heavier weight, mallard were my main choices for retrieving lessons with the younger dog of around nine to twelve months old. Hare, because of its size and weight, I would use nearer the end of the dog's training and then only sparingly, when he proved efficient in carrying normal game. Partridge, because of its reduced scenting properties, would be used for the more difficult retrieves as the dog was nearing the final stages of his retrieving education. Finally, snipe and woodcock would be used and careful observation as to the dog's attitude toward them would be carefully noted, for there are dogs who will flatly refuse to pick these whilst others, with obvious distaste, will carry them. At no time would I advocate using geese for retrieves, either during training or during the dog's first season in the

Springer retrieving woodcock.

shooting field. A little thought should make the reason obvious. If you were asked to pick up an empty plastic bucket, you could do so with thumb and one finger easily. If, on the other hand, you were asked to lift the same bucket full of water, you would be obliged to grip it much tighter. Because of the goose's weight your dog would need to grip the bird more tightly. Too many of these and your dog would develop hard mouth. If a dog is advertised in the press as 'for sale . . . suitable for wildfowler', then it is a safe bet that he has jaws on him like a rat trap.

It goes without saying that frozen game should be thoroughly thawed before a dog is asked to retrieve it. How anyone could contemplate sending a dog for a partially frozen bird is completely beyond me!

Pigeon, because of their loose feathers are particularly distasteful to a young dog, so until such time as the dog displays that he doesn't mind picking up pigeons, in his early experience I would always encase them in nylon tights.

In order to provide as natural a transition as possible, as soon as the individual dog has shown that he is proficient in retrieving game that had been thawed, then, whenever possible he should be presented with the 'cold' stiffened game from the day before. Then after the dog has shown he had no hang-ups regarding these, which he shouldn't, for he will be well and truly grounded in carrying cold game, then I would introduce him to retrieving warm carcases from game shot previously that day.

Retrieving – Encouraging a Good Delivery (Early Training)

There are probably more problems encountered by the trainer in the retrieving department than in any other. When one considers the many pitfalls that lie in wait, that can jeopardise the desired soft mouth of the gundog, it is not at all surprising. Undoubtedly, most dogs who display a problem in retrieving are those who are 'house' as opposed to 'kennel' dogs. Most problems relating to retrieving have been instilled in one way or another by the owner and his family. The children will amuse themselves by constantly throwing uninteresting objects for the puppy to bring back. The obvious danger here is twofold, either they will sicken the puppy so much that he will eventually refuse to pick up, or by pulling and roughly snatching objects out of his mouth they will encourage him to grip. So warn the children that they are not to throw things for him, nor must they chase him around the garden, for therein lies another very common problem. Whilst you the 'trainer' in your spare time are trying to encourage the puppy to come to you, unbeknown to you, the children are busy demonstrating to the puppy the joys of being chased.

Partners, if not enlightened, can be a disturbing element in this respect. If the puppy is kept indoors, you must try to understand their position. A puppy in the house will find, and run about with objects when their back is turned. He has no sense of value, so will chew anything that takes his fancy.

Delivering game to hand.

Your partner, who probably has enough on their plate, in the heat of the moment cannot be expected to exercise canine psychology. The natural reaction is to snatch the object from the puppy's mouth after a frustrating chase around the house. From the pup's point of view, all this is great fun, until he has played your partner up to the extent that in frustration, they belt him one. Such are the trials and tribulations of keeping a pup indoors.

Obviously the puppy must be prepared properly for his future training in the art of retrieving; after all, a gundog that will not retrieve isn't worth much. So, taking the puppy out of his kennel in an area where there are no distractions, allow him to scamper about. As soon as he is on the move, whilst he is still fresh and full of verve, throw a small soft 'dummy' a short distance out in front of him – a sock rolled up is ideal for this as it will have retained scent still on it, although indistinguishable to our senses. It is important that the trainer makes this easy for the pup and lets him see the 'dummy' thrown. He will scamper out eagerly for it. However, do not expect him to come rushing back with it, for his most likely reaction will be to pick it up and go scampering off. Do not alarm him by shouting or indicate by your manner that anything is amiss. Give him two 'peep-peeps' on the plastic return whistle (obviously he will not know what this new sound means, but hopefully it will attract his attention), and repeat this if necessary, whilst at the same time crouch down. In nine cases out of ten he will come running up to the trainer curious at his strange position. The trainer is then afforded the opportunity to hold the puppy, fondle and stroke him, before removing the sock gently from his mouth. Should it be apparent that despite the trainer crouching down and making encouraging noises, the puppy is more intent on shaking and playing with this new interesting object than he is with the trainer, swift unflappable action is required. The trainer must get up from his crouching position, attract the pup's attention and run off slowly away from the pup. The object is not to run *away* from the pup, but to encourage him into thinking that this is what is happening. Once he is coming after his trainer he must be allowed to catch up with him. As soon as the puppy has caught up with the trainer a great fuss must be made of him. At this stage of the game the trainer is not training per se, it is merely a little game. The trainer is laying the foundations, preparing the way for what is to come. Neither should this 'exercise' be overdone; one 'mini' retrieve per session is enough. There are authors who advocate that the puppy is given multiple retrieves along a narrow corridor in his house – it's purely a matter of opinion.

It is important that when the puppy returns to hand with the object, the trainer must convey to him that he is pleased and must not take the 'dummy' from his mouth straight away, but stroke and praise him, before gently removing it from his mouth.

By the trainer's demeanour, the puppy must be encouraged to associate these little interludes as pleasurable. The ease with which he adapts to 'delivering the goods' depends on his temperament and age when these exercises are first introduced into his curriculum. Obviously, if the pup has been bought at six months old, out of a kennel and has had no lessons in carrying, a little more difficulty may be experienced than in a puppy of half that age.

One of the commonest problems concerns the puppy who, perhaps due to an anxiety – eye-shyness (which is much more common than most would think) or a traumatic experience – has associated coming back to the handler with distrust. Such a pup may come back and then either try to rush past or circle around the trainer just out of reach. Whilst this is undoubtedly most aggravating, rather than lose his temper, the trainer would be better advised just to ignore the lesson for that day and return the pup to his kennel in a happy frame of mind. It is then a matter of sitting down and thinking things out. Do not act in haste, the question must be asked – 'why' – there must always be a reason. Perhaps the trainer has done something that may have a bearing on the pup's behaviour. It is probably something very simple, so obvious that the wood cannot be seen for the trees.

If it is suspected that the pup is trying to get past or circle because of anxiety, it must be shown to him that, far from anything to fear, he will be rewarded. In this case be rewarded by praise whenever he comes to hand and not necessarily only when carrying something. Indeed it would not be a bad idea to abandon his little carrying exercises for a week or so until he is

If the handler stands with his back to a wall or similar structure, this will prevent a dog from rushing past on either side or circling whilst retrieving.

freely coming into hand. I have found that with a pup that was wary in coming in to hand, the trick is for the handler to wait until the dog is distracted, lie down on his back in long grass and as soon as he is concealed, attract the pup's attention by 'peeping' the return whistle. Dogs do not like feeling alone and he will come rushing back and discover his handler, who will then shower him with praise. Sounds daft, but it works.

Returning to the retrieving and carrying in to hand. The solution is to make it more difficult for the puppy to get past or circle around his trainer. The best way to achieve this is to stand with your back against a wall, throw the retrieving object straight out in front, crouch down and as soon as the pup has the object, encourage him into hand by voice, whistling, clapping the hands etc.

If whenever an object is thrown for a pup he always runs out, touches it with his nose and then turns and walks off unconcernedly, his behaviour shows a very real problem. This is the classic symptom of a genetically reluc-

Trainer with back to the wall.

tant carrier or, at the very least, the sign of a pup that has been well and truly sickened in relation to picking up. The first case may prove impossible to eradicate, the second may prove to be very difficult; it depends on the degree of abreaction that the pup has undergone, but with experimentation a solution may be found. After due consideration the obvious conclusion is that as the pup is not interested in that particular 'retrieve', a more interesting object must be found.

My reader may think that I have laboured the question regarding early retrieving problems. I have done so, because, as I have said, it is the sphere of retrieving that presents the trainer with more problems than in any other aspect of training, and most retrieving problems are embedded in the dog in his puppyhood.

Retrieving – Forced

When it is considered that even in skilled professional trainers' hands, the ratio of success in this procedure is very low, it is certain then, as far as the amateur trainer is concerned, this is an area of training best left alone. In my view, if a dog is not a natural carrier, the question must be asked, is it worth the trouble to spend good money in 'force retrieving'? My instinct has always been a definite 'No', for this is an aspect of training which in no way carries with it any guarantee of success and therefore, should only be embarked upon as a last desperate effort in remedying a serious retrieving fault. I am aware that there are those trainers who implement this procedure irrespective of whether the dog will retrieve naturally or not. As I have said, this is a practice in which the trainer can by no means be certain of a successful outcome and I cannot see the logic of making life difficult, just for the sake of it.

Advice

The kindest form of forced retrieving in my opinion is quite a simple remedy. I am well aware that there are other methods which involve the dog suffering pain. If a handler cannot find a means whereby the dog can be trained without cruelty, then in my opinion the man would be better to remain dogless. Consequently, I do not intend describing these methods. The commonest type of forced retrieving is simplicity itself. It is merely a case of gently putting a light soft object in the dog's mouth whilst stroking him soothingly, saying 'Hold – Hold – Good Boy – Hold', and whenever he drops it, gently replacing it and repeating 'Hold'. If he shows a marked dislike for the particular object you have chosen, then experiment with several objects until you find one that he will hold.

I once had a springer in for training that had a definite disinclination to pick up anything. By trial and error I finally arrived at the only thing he would hold, a 'canvas dummy' soaked in rabbit scent. I used this until I was sure that his force retrieving was complete. Later I wrapped a rabbit skin around it. Later still, I put mallard wings around it. That's the gundog training business; you must adapt. As soon as the dog has shown that he is willing to hold the dummy for long enough, start walking him on the lead, quietly encouraging him. If he drops it, just quietly replace it, stroking him and repeat, 'Hold – Hold – Good Boy – Hold!'

The natural progression to this regime is to 'Hup' him and throw the favoured object out, not too far initially, then command him to 'Fetch It'. Again he may be reluctant to come back to you and this is one of the times when the check cord can be useful. In the knowledge that he is picking up the object but is reluctant to deliver it, put him onto the check cord, walk him on it for a short time, then order him to 'Hup', throw the object a short way out in front of him and after a few seconds send him for it, dragging the check cord behind him. As soon as he has picked up the object, lift the loose end of the check cord and gradually, slowly (do not get involved in a tug-of-war), bring him into you and make a great fuss of him. Then gently but firmly push the dummy backwards into his mouth and this will encourage him to release it.

Chapter Nineteen

S

Scent

Apart from the huntsman, police dog handler or dog trainer, scent is a subject that does not concern the general public other than perhaps referring to a ladies' perfume and why should it? It is many thousands of years since man had to rely on his nose as a hunter-gatherer to find his prey. The animal instinctively seeks security by its camouflage in the undergrowth and remaining immobile. At the sound of ever-increasing danger approaching, to assist its escape there is a sudden upsurge of glandular activity. Adrenaline, the hormone sometimes referred to as the fight or flight secretion is released. I suspect that it is this hormone that generates the sudden explosion of scent that is released upon the immediate surroundings from the bird or the animal's sudden exit. Scent which is secreted from various glands throughout the animal's body including the anal, in conjunction with the scent from the animal's feet is also quite distinctive to the dog's highly developed sense of smell.

Generally speaking, scent is primarily dependent on the prevailing temperature and movement. If the dog trainer observes a hen pheasant sitting on her nest, he will see that she is invariably facing into the wind. This is because, instinctively she knows that by facing motionless into the wind, she will not give off much, if any, scent which may attract a predator. Although the bird is not aware of it, this is due to the air currents which will pass over her feathers without ruffling them, thereby not much, if any, scent will be released. On the other hand, a pheasant that has been shot and falls tumbling to the ground thus creating maximum wind disturbance through its feathers will leave a heavy pillar of scent which will drift slowly downwind of the fall, depending on the rate of the breeze. In contrast, the pheasant that has been shot and falls straight to the ground with wings closed will afford less scent to the surrounding air currents. Partridge that have been killed in flight will fall to the ground and if they are lying on their back are notoriously difficult for the questing dog to detect especially on bare ground, even in a light breeze. I have seen on various occasions dogs fail on what would appear to be a simple retrieve of a partridge.

As scent is moisture-based, it follows that extremes of temperature will be detrimental to the scenting conditions prevalent at any given time. Therefore, humid warm conditions with a slight breeze would provide ideal scenting conditions, whereas a cold frosty, snow-covered or bare, windy landscape will present very poor scent. Heavy rain will result in poor scenting conditions because the sodden ground will disperse the scent droplets, which will gradually improve as the ground dries. Again within a very small area of ground, scent may vary quite markedly. The shadow side of a hollow where the sun has not as yet struck and is still covered with frost will provide little scope for scent, whereas, only a few yards away on the sunny side of the same hollow where the sun has melted the frost, will show a marked improvement in scent. Sparsely covered ground swept by a stiff breeze will not hold scent for long, whereas only a few metres away where there is more growth the scent-holding properties could be excellent. On the other hand, thick cover will not allow the passage of air through it and consequently will tend to be virtually scentless.

Potency of scent may vary from hour to hour on the same day, to the extent that whilst it may be poor in the morning, depending on the weather, it can improve within a matter of an hour or so. The surrounding terrain can also have a quite marked effect upon scenting conditions. Wet, boggy ground tends to indicate that scent will be sparse because of the fumes that will arise from the bog as the dog hunts through it. This indicates the folly of sending a multitude of dogs onto such ground when pursuing a runner, a not unusual scenario on a formal shooting day. Moist ground that is not of the boggy nature may furnish the dog with excellent scent especially on a mild day. Dry arid conditions are virtually scentless and the scent of game can be swiftly dissipated as it evaporates, even within a few minutes. Vegetation, or lack of, will affect scent. Also the types of plant growth may be such as to give off pungent scent in their own right. For instance wild garlic will with great efficiency cloud any scent provided by a passing animal. A hillside banked with gorse in full bloom will have an obstructive effect on scent as will rotting ground vegetation.

Scent is contained within moist air droplets, consequently the more turbulent activity in the air, the more scent will be released and spread over an area, depending on strength of the wind and the prevailing conditions, thereby providing the dog with a guide to his quarry. As I have indicated, bare ground will be quickly swept clean of any scent, whereas plant growth may contain it for some considerable time. I remember a classic specific incidence of this.

I was at a field trial where the first few dogs called in to the line were required to hunt under tall rhododendron bushes which skirted a large lawn at the front of the house. There had been a light shower of rain which had given way to a rather stiff following wind. A bird was flushed, shot and came crashing down through the heavy foliage and made a run for it. My dog was sent after it and aiding him as much as I could, my vision being obstructed by the foliage, I managed to get him close to the fall. From that moment on, the proceedings were nothing more than a disaster. Could I get him on to the line? Not a chance! A couple of times I managed to 'sheep dog' him on to the general direction from where I thought the bird had made its getaway, but each time he came back, nose up in the low lying foliage. The next dog also failed on what was a very difficult task, for the moisture-laden foliage held the scent from the bird's descent for quite a considerable time. In comparison, the bare ground beneath the bushes where the scent droplets had been dissipated, rapidly loses the scent in the following breeze. Scent is distinctly different between the various species of game. Any experienced dog man will have noticed that their experienced dogs have a different body language as they approach and work up to specific game, to the extent that it is apparent to his trainer what type of game is about to be flushed.

On a frosty morning, a rabbit that has been sitting cosily overnight within his little tussock of grass, providing he does not break cover, will be virtually undetectable until the questing dog's nose is within a few inches from him. The rabbit who sits motionless can be very difficult for a dog to find. Indeed, I couldn't count the amount of times that I have been disqualified from a field trial for missing tightly seated rabbits. Such has been the plight of all field trial competitors, if they care to admit it. However, the flighty rabbit who upon hearing the dogs approach, loses his nerve and bolts, the sudden explosion of scent droplets released around him at his swift departure immediately provides strong scent which will be detected by the dog at quite a few metres distance.

It is important for the reader to realise that there are two methods in which scent may be spread. One is by 'air scent', as with the tumbling pheasant and the other is 'ground scent' which is left by game that has passed over the ground. The degree of potency presented to a questing dog will depend greatly upon the prevailing scent conditions and how much time has passed since the scent carrier had released the air or ground scent as it made its fall through the air or its journey over the ground. The dog which is working on 'air scent' will be seen to have his nose up and depending on the stiffness of the breeze to be working a 'line' quite a few feet downwind along the line or source of the scent. A dog working on ground scent will be seen to react differently to the dog on air scent. He will have his nose to the ground and occasionally may be heard to make a snuffling noise, whilst his speed will vary as he quarters his ground quite quickly, then hesitating for a brief moment, perhaps where a pocket of scent seems stronger at a given spot, then moving on working quite vigorously at speed, displaying extremely excited body language. As he gets ever closer to the quarry his pattern of hunting will narrow until, upon finding the game, there is a last savage forward thrust as he pushes the game out of its sanctuary.

As scent is completely dependent upon the temperature and air currents surrounding it, it follows that as hot air rises the same physical rule will apply to the scent droplets contained within it. As the scent rises in the warm air currents, rather like a pillar of smoke, will waft downwind. In a strong wind these scent droplets will be quickly dispersed and therefore within a very short space of time, leave little evidence for the dog to follow. The experienced handler is acutely aware that he needs to get his dog into the 'fall' area as rapidly as possible in the knowledge that if too much time elapses before his dog 'winds' the bird, the chances of a successful collection of the bird will rapidly deteriorate.

Dogs react quite markedly to the prevailing scenting conditions. A dog with a good nose, working in poor scenting conditions, will be noticed by his handler to be working much more slowly than his usual hunting pace as he thoroughly investigates his ground. Such a dog will find game: he is a 'gamefinder'. Scenting conditions good or bad will make little or no difference to a dog with a poor nose. He will traverse his ground at his usual speed in a monotonous windscreen-wiper action and with his nose up. Such a dog will produce little game, other than that which bursts from cover at the sound of his approach. Nose is of paramount importance in the working gundog. A dog with a poor nose is of no use to the shooting man and is best got rid of.

Undoubtedly the best season of the year for providing good scenting conditions is the autumn, for the heavy scent disguising summertime blossoms have gone, as has the scent-consuming heat of the sun. Early spring may not be as fruitful as the autumn for good scenting conditions, however it is far more conducive to good scenting conditions than the winter months.

In the final analysis at a field trial, more often than not the judges are left to determine the awards by re-examining a few dogs in what is known as the run-off. Nor does it follow that the winner of the stake is among them, for he might well be termed as 'on the shelf' and will therefore not compete in the final run-off. The few dogs chosen by the judges will be brought in turn in front of them for their final assessment. Usually two dogs will be run together for comparison, but occasionally one dog will be selected by the judges to run on its own. In such circumstances it would be easy for those left as spectators in the 'gallery' to think that the upshot of the trial would be determined on an excellent retrieve of perhaps a runner. As the dogs involved in the run-off have already shown the judges their prowess in every aspect of their work in the trial earlier in the day, a retrieve in the run-off should have no effect upon the final results. Naturally if a specific dog is unlucky enough to commit a disqualifying fault, then he will be discarded. The efficient judge may be interested in reassuring himself on comparing style and speed between two or three dogs. However, at the end of the day he will be looking for the dog most likely to find game. For all the retrieving, steadiness, style and pace in the dog's performance is of little importance if a hunting dog cannot find game, and the handler would be wise to get rid of him, for he is not worth a candle! It would be far more sensible for him to seek another pup in the hope that he will be luckier the second time around.

Sheep Dogging (Intermediate & Advanced Training)

This is the rather derogatory label given to the hand and whistle signals which are used in guiding the dog at distance to a 'blind' retrieve, a bird which has fallen unmarked by the dog. My reader will note that I have indicated that this guidance is perfectly in order when handling the dog out to an unseen bird. Provided that the handler gives the guidance quietly, I would never penalise him. On the other hand, I hold strongly to the view that a dog that requires this kind of guidance to ground game which he has found himself is not worth his keep. I would allow a minimum of guidance to a dog called in to collect ground game that had been flushed by another dog. The guidance I would permit would be to allow the handler to guide his dog to the vacant seat. Thereafter the dog should be left to his own devices.

Shot – Dropping to (Intermediate Training)

There is nothing difficult in this. Once the dog is proficient in dropping to the whistle and hand signals and shows no fear of the starter pistol, it is a simple matter to practise dropping to shot in conjunction with the voice or whistle command. A point worth noting in regard to this exercise is that the

Grouse away and this Irish setter drops to wing.

crack of the starter pistol is distinctly different from the duller tone of the dummy launcher, both of which are significantly different from the shotgun report.

Upon embarking upon a lesson involving shot of any kind, the trainer must consider the location where he intends to train the dog in relation to the shot. In the dog's earliest training pertaining to shot, under no circumstances discharge a shot, whether by starter pistol, dummy launcher or shotgun, near to buildings, beside heavy woodland, in a deep valley or anywhere where you think an echo may be produced.

Ideally, as with all training, I advocate that a natural progression is made in each stage of the dog's education. The trainer will determine in advance the young dog's attitude to shot before embarking upon the following training regime. The starter pistol would be the first choice in introducing the young dog to shot, then after a suitable period of training, once it is obvious that the dog has no hang-ups regarding the pistol shot, the trainer would introduce the dummy launcher, thereafter gradually the shot from the shotgun would be employed. It may seem to be stating the obvious, but I believe that it is better to be safe than sorry, therefore lessons pertaining to the sound of the shot must be used sparingly at all times. Do not fire a fusillade of shots over a young dog. This is also a small but important point

Dropping to shot – a brace of pointers at a field trial.

to make: a dog must never be seated immediately in front of the gun, for he will get the full force of the shot over his head.

To the procedure then. Hunt the dog as you would usually do and when you think it convenient to drop him whilst he is hunting, raise your hand in the 'Hup' mode, give the 'thunderer' stop whistle signal whilst simultaneously discharging the starter pistol. The dog will, if you have schooled him properly and not rushed things, drop like a stone. Initially upon commencing with any 'new' approach to training, the young dog will respond to the familiar signal, the one that he has grown accustomed to, but in time, through association he will gradually respond to the new signal as well. As time goes on, he will drop to the shot alone. Nevertheless as usual, it is better to play safe and give the whistle signal at all times. A good maxim with all training is moderation in all things. This is especially important with the stop whistle and drop to shot lesson. Do not be continually stopping and dropping the dog to shot whilst he is hunting, otherwise you will confuse him, even to the point that he will become a 'sticky' hunter. If the trainer dropped the dog once to the hand/whistle signal and then, once more to the hand, whistle and shot, in other words, twice in one training session, then to my mind that is sufficient for one day. Providing the trainer is consistent, it would be reasonable to expect that this lesson would be thoroughly bedded into the dog within a matter of weeks.

Sighted Retrieves (Early & Intermediate Training)

The sighted or marked retrieve is usually given in the early stages of the dog's training, its main purpose being to illustrate to the pupil that it is there and thereby encourage him. In the later stages of training, it would normally be used in the more complicated obedience lessons as a distraction, perhaps in conjunction with an unmarked retrieve, on land or water, when it would be intended that the dog be encouraged to ignore the obvious retrieve and go for the hidden dummy. In time, the sighted retrieve will be used in building the dog's trust in you and your commands, so that he will accept them even when he has not marked a retrieve. It is in making the early retrieves easy, then progressively more difficult as the dog's training advances, that enhances that trust in him, and it is because of the importance of this that initially the dog must not fail.

When the puppy is only twelve or fourteen weeks old, the sighted retrieve is an old sock or similar item which is thrown only sixty or ninety centimetres away on a grassy lawn. This is obviously the embryonic stage of the retrieving lessons that he will be given in his future training and as with all 'carrying' lessons must not be overdone.

Later, perhaps at four or five months old, during exercise a proper dummy will be used and thrown much further, but still within sight of the dog. At this point in the dog's preparation for his training yet to come, some hint in steadiness to the dummy may or may not be used. I am quite ambivalent concerning this. I have always left this aspect until later, perhaps six months old, before I started to teach obedience concerning steadiness to the thrown dummy. Other trainers prefer to initiate a hint of steadiness to the thrown dummy earlier. As I have said, I do not have any objection to this. But above all I insist on utility in retrieving exercises at all times. Never forget that after the first few retrieves, the novelty will have worn off as far as the dog is concerned and thereafter, even though he appears to be enthusiastic, he is merely obeying your command to retrieve – more as his duty to obey your wishes. There are many dogs who will obey the command to fetch a dummy throughout their entire lives, but then there are those who will draw the line much earlier, even whilst still undergoing their training, and refuse to retrieve the dummy. In such cases you have manufactured your problem. So, be safe, ration the dummy retrieving.

Initially the early introduction to a hint of steadiness to the thrown dummy, is to hold the puppy by the scruff of the neck and chuck the dummy out to the front in clear view of him. As you will be crouched down whilst doing this, it stands to reason that the distance you can throw the dummy is limited quite significantly. That is of no matter, for at this stage of the game everything must be made easy for the pup. He must succeed. The trainer will then release the puppy and let it scamper out. Usually, upon their picking up this new and interesting object they will shake it and want to play with it. Crouching down, the trainer will clap his hands quietly, merely to attract the puppy's attention and make encouraging sounds or whistle to bring him back to hand. No attempt should be made to remove the object from his mouth when he comes into hand, for he will be reluctant to surrender his prized object to you. If you attempt to remove it from his mouth, this may encourage him to grip and thereby hard mouth may be induced and at the very least make the dog reluctant to approach you. Remember, he learns by association, so a pleasant experience in carrying is to be recommended. By associating his coming in to the trainer as a pleasant experience, he will soon return to you with his dummy enthusiastically. Upon his coming into hand, praise him, fondle him and tickle him, then, very gently push the dummy back up into his mouth. He will then open his jaws and release it quite easily. It will not be very long before the dummy loses its interest and is no longer his reason for coming in to the trainer and he will drop the retrieved object readily into the trainer's hand.

Stinking Out

Not a very glamorous title, I agree, but it hides a trade secret not known as a rule by the normal, run of the mill, shooting man.

We are all aware that in spite of the rabbit's apparently miraculous resurrection from almost total annihilation during the onset of the devastating, man-made plague, myxomatosis, that there appear to be spells of resurrection in its virulence and a variance in the rabbit's immunity.

There appear to be regular intervals throughout each season when the infection raises its ugly head once more with apparent equal severity within the rabbit population in the area, soon to die down again and the small conies to appear again shortly after. Nevertheless, to those of us old enough to remember the introduction to this country of this disease, the present-day infections are mild and obviously the rabbit has to a great extent built up an immunity. The infection is transported from rabbit to rabbit by a parasitic flea, which in the act of biting the rabbit, injects its bloodstream with the infection. As I have said, the successful gundog trainer has to be aware of and act accordingly to many circumstances, many actions of which to some might appear bizarre, even highly amusing.

Such an incident happened one day when my friend Tom Laird arrived at my kennels to find me in the act of delousing some rabbits that I had transported from a local ground intending to put them in the pen.

Tom: 'What are you doing?'

Me: 'I'm delousing these rabbits in case they have the "mixi" bug, before I put them into the pen.'

Tom, solemnly: 'Get away, I would never have thought of that!'

Everyone in the field trial world had the greatest respect and love for Tom. He was an unrivalled raconteur, but he had a dreadful memory, so bad that I am quite certain it must have landed him in many embarrassing situations.

At a field trial a few days later, Tom was recounting with great glee, an encounter he had had a few days earlier with a man who he had discovered delousing rabbits before he put them into the rabbit pen. When he had finished his amusing tale the tears were streaming down his face, and I said, 'That's right Tom, the man was me!'

To this Tom never even batted an eyelid, saying, 'Well, there you are, y'see. It just goes to show that we're always learning.'

The fact that this disease has had such a devastating effect upon the rabbit population of the UK is only relevant to those directly involved in farming and to a much lesser extent the shooting man.

When I was young in the 'pre-mixi' days, the sight of the 'rabbit-man' walking his bicycle, festooned and almost totally hidden by rabbits was a common sight along our country lanes. The price received for them, I seem to recall was two and a half new pence (sixpence old money) a brace. Alas, another small vestige of the traditional British country life has disappeared, for such colourful country folk no longer exist.

The fact that rabbits are plentiful or not, as I have said is of major importance to the farmer and his living. Those of us not old enough to remember cannot possibly imagine just how devastating the rabbit activity was upon the crops of those times. I have seen fields with young shoots of grain cropped clean for five metres around its boundaries.

Then there is the shooting man. Generally his motives are different and if he happens to be a field trial enthusiast then it is of paramount importance that he will be able to provide his dogs with sufficient ground game if he is to entertain any thought of success in these affairs, especially if they are based in Scotland. To him the desperate farmer can be a godsend.

Both the farmer and the shooting man can work together in this however, by 'stinking out'. The procedure is simplicity itself and merely entails some legwork. At each burrow complex, a piece of sacking measuring approximately ten by ten centimetres, soaked in Creosote or old engine oil is thrust as far down the burrow as can be reached. The same treatment is meted out to all the other burrows in the complex, leaving only a few burrows clear as escape routes.

To be most effective in clearing the rabbits out to sleep in the open, approximately four to five days should be left before shooting the area. If your evacuation scheme has worked, you will find the rabbit population sitting out and easy targets as they bolt for the burrows to be instantly repelled from each by the pungent overpowering smell.

Substitute Judges

Field trials as a rule are held during the shooting season, the winter. This means that field trialists spend much of their time in long-distance travelling, very often in the early hours of the morning, during the most dangerous and worst weather conditions of the year. Without appearing too dramatic, a little thought will illustrate that, in fact, the trial competitor is putting his own safety at risk in order to attend these affairs. I have been involved in more than one accident through the years due to bad weather conditions en route to a trial, or returning from one. Added to the obvious perils on the road, is the expense in travelling sometimes hundreds of miles. On the other hand, very often if it is a two-day trial, a stay in a hotel will be necessary, which is anything but inexpensive.

When a member of a field trial society receives notice of an impending trial, he or she will decide whether they wish to enter for the draw. This decision will be strongly affected by the judges that have been elected by the field trial committee to officiate at the trial. These competitors deserve the respect of the field trial committee.

It is by no means unusual for the field trial competitor, upon arriving on the morning of a trial to find that one of the judges is a substitute. Neither is it unusual to hear from some that if they had known that so-and-so was going to judge they would not have considered applying for a draw. When all is considered, the potential danger in travelling great distances in the winter, the travelling and hotel expenses, I feel that the trialists deserve better. This is a bone of contention with most field trialists, yet it need not happen, for the solution is clear – after selection of the judges has taken place at the field trial committee meeting, two more should be chosen as reserve judges, to stand by and replace an absent judge.

Chapter Twenty

T

Taking Signalled Directions at Distance (Intermediate & Advanced Training)

Sometimes this is also contemptuously referred to as 'sheep dogging'. This rather derogatory label is apportioned to the hand and whistle signals which are utilised in guiding the dog at distance to a blind retrieve, a bird that has fallen unmarked by the dog. The reader will note that I have indicated that this 'guidance' is perfectly in order when handling the dog out to an unseen bird, where for humanitarian reasons a rapid recovery is desired. In such circumstances, providing the handler gives the signals without too much noise, I would never penalise him. On the other hand, I am strongly of the view that a dog which requires this kind of assistance to ground game that he has found himself, is not worth his salt. I would allow a minimum of guidance to a dog called in to collect ground game that had been flushed by another dog and shot. The guidance that I would permit would be to allow the handler to guide his dog to the vacant seat. Thereafter the dog should be

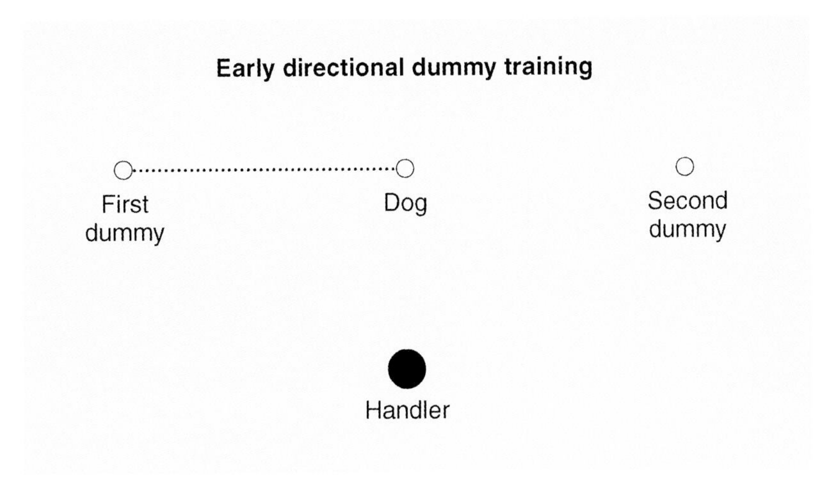

Early directional dummy training.

left to his own devices as he should be fully capable of taking a line to the wounded game. A dog that has never been taught to take a line cannot be considered to be fully trained.

The Three Ladies (Intermediate & Advanced Training)

This exercise is the forerunner to the dog's future shooting days when he will be expected to trust, accept unquestioningly and act upon directions given to him at distance, whether it be on land or in water. If the trainer has any hope of training his dog to a good standard, then these lessons are extremely important.

Because no two dogs are alike, whenever a new lesson is introduced the trainer must expect that each dog may react to this new demand upon him in different ways. Some dogs appear to take to each new lesson like a duck to water, almost as though they had been born before. In marked contrast, others may appear to be obtuse or just downright stubborn, uncooperative and apparently more difficult and slow to learn. Experience has taught me that it is by no means unusual for the apparent 'star', our young prodigy, for no apparent reason, to suddenly break down and present the trainer with unforeseen problems. I feel sure these are quite simply a case of, quick to pick it up, quick to forget. In marked contrast, it is not at all unusual for the dog that appeared initially to be slow on the uptake to suddenly blossom and in the due course of time to mature into a far superior dog than his more boisterous and confident companion.

This facet of training is only embarked upon after the dog has proved that he is one hundred per cent efficient in the 'Get Out' or 'Go Back' retrieving lessons to the unseen retrieve.

As always, the following lesson is a natural progression to what has gone before. Prior to bringing the dog out of his kennel, go to the area that you

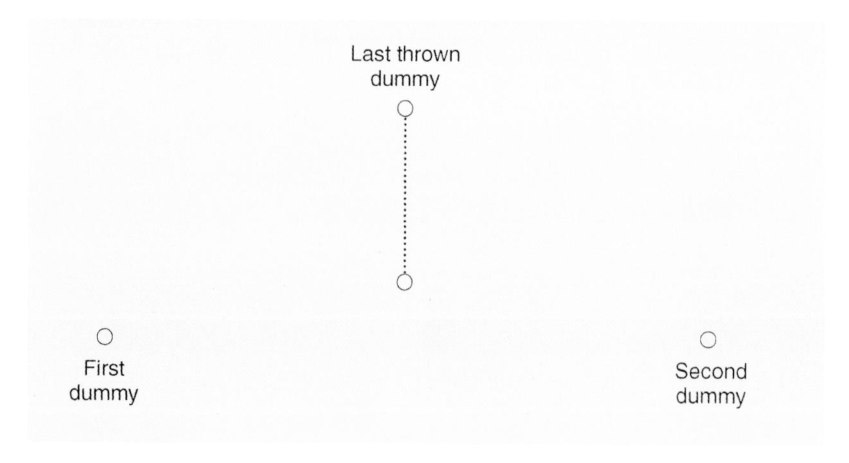

The three ladies.

have chosen for that day's training session and walking into the wind throw two dummies a short distance apart, straight out in front of you. Turning downwind from these, retrace your steps for approximately five metres and mark the spot where you intend to drop the dog, anything will do, a peg or a cigarette packet, anything that comes to hand, then go and get the dog.

Hunt him for some distance, progressing toward the 'mark'. When he reaches it, drop him as close as possible to that spot. Keep him sitting there, then with the verbal 'Go Back' or 'Get Out', accompanied by the distinct hand signal, send him for one of the concealed dummies. It does not matter which dummy he brings to hand, for the object is to get success rapidly.

Next comes the progression. Sit him back on the spot, walk back for about six to eight paces, pause, then, throw a dummy to land about four metres at right angles to him, it doesn't matter which side of him you choose. Pause again, keeping your eye on him, then, with a clear verbal command 'Get Out' or 'Go Back', accompanied once again by the clear hand signal, send him for the one remaining unseen dummy. It will not be surprising if he attempts to go for the dummy that he knows is there but you must discourage this. The aim is to build the dog's trust in you. He must learn that if you indicate something that he has not seen, then it is there. Once you have succeeded on a sufficient number of occasions with this exercise then we may move on, again in a natural progression.

During the routine training period, the dog will be brought to a halt by the stop whistle, combined with the distinct hand signal at a distance of approximately four metres in front of the trainer. The canvas dummy is thrown in full view of him, to land approximately, five to six metres at right angles to the dog's seated position. Keep him steady on the drop, even if this requires extra hand-signal endorsement for a few moments, then with the appropriate distinct hand signal and vocal 'Dead There' or 'Hi Lost' whichever is preferred, send him for the dummy. With such a simple task no problems should be encountered.

The natural progression to this is to hunt him on again, as you would normally in the general exercise routine for a short time, then drop him again with the hand signal and drop whistle. This time throw a canvas dummy to land at right angles to his left, keeping him steady to the drop. Wait for a few seconds then cast the second dummy to land at right angles to his right. Again wait for an appropriate period, keeping him steady, then again with the appropriate distinct hand signal and this time a single 'peep' from the turn whistle, send him for the dummy to his left. The young dog's natural inclination will be to go for the dummy last thrown, the one to his right. In the initial stages of these new lessons, be ready, expect him to attempt to go for the last dummy thrown and stop him as soon as his intentions are clear.

Occasionally, depending upon just how reliable he is on the drop whistle, you may fail to stop him. Do not make a big thing of this. As soon as you see that he has the dummy in his mouth, you have no alternative. Remember under no circumstances must the trainer chastise or scold a dog whilst he is in the act of carrying something. Just call him into hand with the two little sharp 'peep-peeps' on the return whistle and accept the dummy. Hunt him on again for a short while, then repeat the procedure. Do not persevere with this lesson overmuch, don't forget, retrieving training must always be kept to a minimum, in order not to bore the dog. After a couple of attempts, if you are still not successful, then give him one last easy retrieve and take him home. There's always tomorrow.

If on the next day you are still not successful, then you must be prepared to accept that, if upon embarking on any new lesson it is proving to be problematic, then it is likely that the training fault lies, not in the new tuition, but in the last appropriate lesson pertaining to the problem that you are now experiencing. In this particular instance, either the directional whistle, hand signal, the stop whistle or even all three lessons have not been sufficiently absorbed, indicating that you are probably rushing it. The trainer must at all stages of training be prepared to accept that sometimes as in this instance, revision is indicated. Don't forget, this is not a race.

Once you have him working well with the two dummies, it will be time to introduce him to the three dummies. But remember, make haste slowly or you may live to regret it. As with the last lesson, the trainer will throw out the two dummies at right angles to the seated dog, one to each side of him, keeping him steady to each. The new variation is the addition of the third dummy, making doubly sure at this particular time that you keep a special eye on the dog, keeping him steady.

What is likely to happen? As soon as you have thrown the second dummy, the dog will be hyping himself up to go at your next command, for he is not to know that you are about to throw another dummy. A good trainer is the one who is always one step ahead of his dog. The third dummy is thrown straight out in front of you over the dog's head, to land perhaps three to four metres behind him. Keeping your hand up in the stop mode, keep him lying there for a few seconds longer then, with a clear forward motion of your hand, command him to 'Go Back' or 'Get out' whichever is preferred, then send him for the last dummy thrown, the one behind him. Remember this, once a particular signal, whether by voice, whistle or hand is chosen, for the rest of the dog's life it must be adhered to. Never ever fire a volley of different commands at a dog: remember his limited reasoning powers.

From now on, in the general daily exercise period, you will be able to ring the changes, until such times that upon your command he shows that he is efficient in all aspects of 'the three ladies'.

Tracking or Taking a Line (Intermediate & Advanced Training)

It is essential that the gundog must be taught to 'take a line', even if it is only for humanitarian purposes, for he cannot be considered to be fully trained if he is incapable of following an air or a foot scent in order to collect a runner.

The ability to take a line to a runner varies greatly from one dog to another, even between litter brothers and sisters. On occasion I have been asked, what was the best spaniel on taking a line that I ever had. I would be hard put to choosing between F.T.W. Macsiccar Merrit and F.T.W. Macsiccar Michele. If asked what was the best spaniel on a runner that I had ever seen, I would probably say Tom Laird's F.T.Ch. Criffel Cherry, Merrit's mother. However to guard against being biased, I would have to admit that George Drummond's bitch F.T.Ch. Drumbro Daisy would have run 'Cherry' pretty closely.

In preparing to lay a line, the trainer's main object is to avoid leaving his foot scent for the dog to follow, for there is no doubt about it, the dog recognises his trainer's scent beyond any other. Far fetched though it may seem, but I assure my reader it is true, during my pipe-smoking era, I once lost my pipe in the snow whilst training a dog on the Burrance moor in January. Two months later, in April, whilst hunting a young dog, impatiently, I signalled him to get on, for I was sure that he was pottering. He came towards me obviously in the retrieving mode, and laid my pipe in my hand.

There is nothing difficult in preparation for this particular aspect of the dog's education. Indeed, in comparison to when I trained my first few dogs there are now training aids that did not exist in those days, which make the task much simpler.

As I have previously mentioned, the 'dummy launcher' utilising the 'launcher ball' smeared with the appropriate animal or bird scent, has

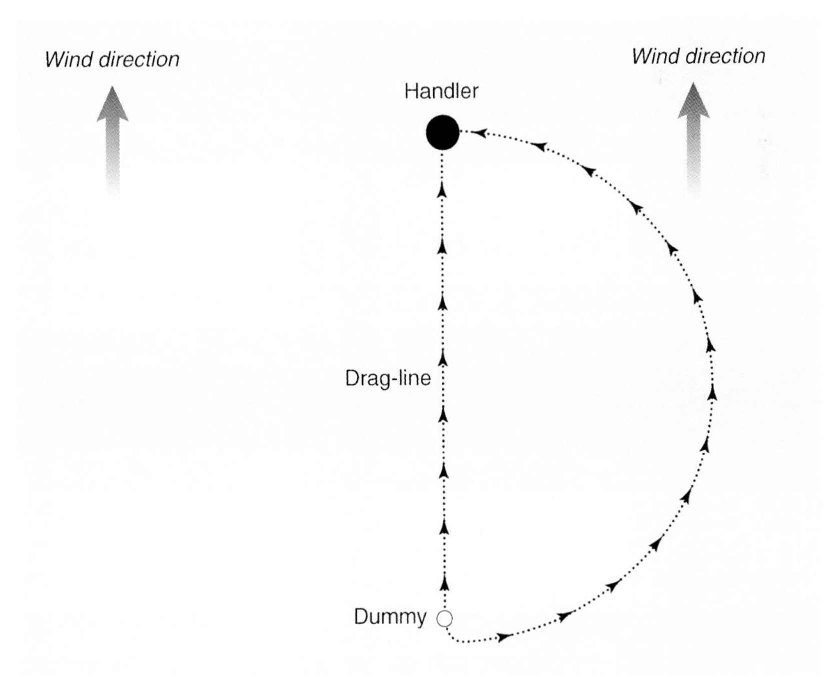

Laying a drag line.

transformed the task of laying a line that could never have been envisaged in my early years and made it so much easier, saving on the trainer's legwork, as well as giving the dog a realistic scent to follow. The ball will, once launched, not only provide the dog with practice in marking the 'fall', it will roll on for a considerable distance, depending on the terrain, thereby providing a 'line' for the dog to follow.

But now to the 'old-fashioned' way. Some trainers prefer to introduce this lesson at an earlier stage in the dog's training by using the normal dummy covered with a rabbit skin to lay the line. Others would use a dummy smeared with aniseed. I prefer to wait until such times as the dog is accustomed to carrying the real thing. Each to his own method; it is purely a matter of opinion and the individual's choice.

Taking a rabbit or a bird (I preferred the rabbit for this because of its stronger scent) I would attach a strong cord approximately ten metres long, around its waist. I would then walk downwind away from the rabbit paying out the line as I went. Once I had arrived at the end of the cord, holding the line taut I would take a right-angle turn and still keeping a tight line I would complete a semi-circle, until I was in a straight line directly upwind of the rabbit. It was then merely a matter of pulling the rabbit's carcase up to me and disengaging the line from it. This provides the dog with a 'drag line'. The object of this procedure is to avoid leaving your familiar foot scent for the dog to follow, for he will recognise your foot scent and tend to follow it instead of the 'drag line' and therefore through your carelessness you have defeated your purpose, which is to teach the pup to recognise and follow the scent of the rabbit.

Again, as an alternative, some trainers will enlist the help of a friend and with perhaps five metres of cord between each of them, with the rabbit in the middle, they would lay the line for perhaps initially ten metres, gradually at intervals throughout the rest of the dog's training increasing the distance.

The scent of the rabbit alone is not enough though, for the dog would not learn to differentiate between the wounded game scent (I prefer to call it 'powder scent', *see* page 9) and the normal scents that abound on the shoot. This would make him tend to follow willy-nilly, every game scent that he encountered, thus destroying his hunting pattern, which as I have explained is known as 'lining' – a most undesirable trait. In an attempt to provide the dog with, as they believe a 'blood' scent, there are trainers who will, prior to laying the line, slash the rabbit's guts. I can think of no better way to teach a young dog to grip and thereby, if persevered with, develop into 'hard mouth'. My solution to teaching the young dog to recognise the difference between game that has been shot, as opposed to the unshot game which he must ignore whilst in pursuit of a runner, is to hold my starter pistol close into the rabbit's carcase and fire a couple of shots before commencing with laying the line.

Training Collars

There is one training aid which I have never used and that is the 'electronic collar'. Having said that, many trainers work well with them but I prefer to use other methods as described below.

I have on many occasions seen a dog drop to the flush before the handler had put any pressure on the restraining cord or used the electronic collar, yet subsequently once in the open was as wild as a hawk when finding a rabbit. The answer to this should be obvious. The dog knows when it is wearing the check cord or electronic collar and when he is not.

Advice

Be fleet of foot. That one little sentence explains the secret of training a dog. On one occasion I used a check cord. If my memory serves me right the trial lasted about ten minutes before I cast it aside, for it was an absolute nuisance.

In training your dog in steadiness, you must decide whether at that point in time, you want to be a shooter or a dog trainer. If you want to be a dog trainer you are defeated at the outset if you take a gun with you, for it is very tempting to be diverted from your dog's actions by trying a pot-shot at a fleeing rabbit and it is in that microsecond whilst your attention is elsewhere that your dog will break. If you possess a rabbit pen then, well and good, if you do not, then it is of little importance, for in the pen or out of it I trained all my dogs in exactly the same way. All that you require is vigilance. Be aware of your dog; never take your eyes off him, for it is in that one unguarded moment that Murphy's law will put the rabbit up in front of your inexperienced dog. Most importantly, work the dog in a very close tight quartering pattern no more than three metres each side of you and no more than two metres in front at all times. Here you are 'loading the dice in your favour'.

Generally speaking, as your dog, no matter how inexperienced he may be, approaches the rabbit's seat there will be a marked change in his behaviour. The closer he gets to the 'seat' the stronger the scent will become and the busier your dog's body language will become, thereby you are forewarned of the impending find and the flush. With an inexperienced dog the advantage is with the handler, for although he is getting progressively more excited with the scent, this is purely instinctive. He has yet to learn where the source of this smell is coming from. When he eventually finds the source, the flush is immediate, creating a momentary instant of surprise for the dog. We know that a dog in full flight is pretty near impossible to catch, however, in the act of the find there is hesitation and for a few seconds, total surprise in the dog. It is in that brief moment that the trainer should be able to steal the initiative from his dog by calling him to drop with the stop whistle. If he is in the act of actually breaking, the dog will not be travelling at full throttle. At the first flush of a rabbit, he is easily caught and restrained, even on the second or third find. However from then on be doubly vigilant for the element of surprise in the dog is waning to the extent that at any time now he will break and if you have not got a reasonable degree of steadiness in him by then, you could be in for some problems. In such a case, remember, if difficulty is being experienced by the trainer with any new aspect of training, then it is indicative that the problem lies in the previous relevant step in the dog's education, in this particular instance, the stop whistle.

Trust Your Dog

This is akin to 'game sense' insofar as it is closely related. Obviously during the dog's training and during his first season's shooting, the trainer is wise to err on the side of caution. However there comes a time when the dog has gained enough experience, that a certain amount of trust must be allocated to him.

I had this salutary lesson taught to me in my early field trial days. I was hunting Field Trial Winner Macsiccar Santa Sue, one of my early dogs, a very stylish hunter with an excellent nose who, due to an early death only managed to win one field trial. It was also the first encounter I had with the legendary Jack Windle, owner of the world renowned 'Jordieland strain', who was judging.

Sue flushed a cock pheasant approximately five metres in front of me. The bird had only reached a height of perhaps seven metres when I could clearly see that it was hit by my right-hand gun. Almost immediately thereafter it was hit again, this time by the gun on my left and fell approximately ten or twelve metres in front of me in heavy cover. Well at such close range what would you have thought? Convinced that the bird must be dead and noting that Sue had marked the fall, I was confident of an easy retrieve. On the judge's command I sent her. She dashed into the cover and to my horror the next glimpse I had of her she was away out to my left about fifty to sixty metres away. In a panic I stopped her by whistle then sent her back to the 'fall'. Again she turned and careered off in the same direction. Once more I brought her back to where I was convinced the dead bird must be. The quiet voice behind me asked me to stop the dog. Jack then enquired as to what I was doing. I explained that I was trying to get her onto the dead bird. He told me that the bird was not dead and was in fact a very strong 'runner' and that he would give me one last chance on it. After what seemed an eternity to me I saw her coming back with the bird which had its head down. As I took the bird from her I noticed that there were strands of bracken in her mouth. Jack examined the bird and then told me to put the lead on.

At the end of the trial I was sitting at the back of my car, taking my boots off and preparing to go home when I became aware of Jack's presence standing at the side of the car. He remarked that he had been watching me at several trials and that he was very impressed by the standard of training that my dogs displayed. He also remarked that I would have to learn to trust my dogs and that if I had allowed the dog to take the line on her first attempt that she would have caught the runner before it had had the time to get firmly tucked into the reeds. It was because the bird had managed to secure good cover that the dog was forced to exert pressure to free the bird and thereby put its ribs in. It was a lesson that I never forgot and the beginning of a long friendship.

Trust Yourself

Faith in your own capabilities in what should be a simple task, the training of your dog, is just as important as trusting your dog. There are many

Faith in your own capabilities is important.

training aids now available to the aspiring gundog trainer, the greatest majority being innocuous enough. To the professional trainer many may be considered unnecessary. However in my view, if purchasing a particular piece of training equipment helps the novice trainer either in the practical or psychological sense then I would regard it as a good and sensible buy.

Chapter Twenty-One

U

Unmarked Retrieves (Intermediate & Advanced Training)

The purpose of this exercise is merely to familiarise the dog with the 'Get Out' or 'Go Back' vocal signal, in conjunction with the appropriate hand signal.

As this is the first variation from the normal routine when the dog has marked his retrieve, it is essential that rapid success is achieved. Initially the dummy should be dropped only a short distance from where you plan to drop the dog. It is essential in order to ensure success with the first few retrieves, that they are made as simple as possible, for it is most undesirable that the dog has to start hunting overlong to find the dummy, for initially he has no idea what he is looking for so he may quickly become discouraged.

I have found that by far the simplest way to achieve this is to choose a day when the wind will be on my back and whilst walking along the boundary wall, with the dog scampering in front of me, without the dog being aware of it, I would drop a dummy behind me. Without stopping, I would keep walking for approximately four to six metres. The dog would then be dropped by whistle and hand signal in front of me. Walking quietly up to him, I would praise him and then standing back, this time upwind of him, I would give a distinctive forward motion, even an exaggerated hand signal with the verbal command 'Get Out' or 'Go Back', indicating the direction along the side of the wall that I wished him to take. Some hesitation by the pup would by no means be unusual, for this is a completely new pursuit for him and he is not sure of what you want from him. To a degree there is always a period of uncertainty whenever a new aspect of training is introduced. By design we are working into the wind and with the aid of the wall and not forgetting the aid afforded the dog by your familiar foot scent, it should not be too difficult for the pup to 'wind' the dummy as it is only a short distance from him. Initially the handler may need to emphasise the hand signal by repeating it whilst stepping forward.

This is quite a simple lesson and in no time at all, you will be able to increase the distance along the wall between the unseen dummy and the dog, in conjunction with stationing your position increasingly further from the sitting dog and from where you wish to give him the 'Get Out' command. It should not be long before the young dog recognises the hand signal and the verbal command and from then on you will be able to dispense with the wall as an aid.

The training is advancing all the time and each new lesson is incorporated with the usual training regime in as natural a format as possible. The natural progression to the unseen dummy exercise with the wall as an aid, is as below.

Unseen Multiple Dummies (Intermediate & Advanced Training)

Before taking the dog out for that particular day's training, you must prepare for it in the following manner. Walking into the wind, go to the area where you intend to give him his lesson. Standing still, facing the wind, throw several dummies in an arc as far as you can. Start his tuition for the day a suitable distance from where you have planted the dummies, so that you can implement various facets of his training to date as you approach the area.

Once you are confident that he is near the spot where the dummies landed, stop him with the whistle and hand signal. Keep him on the drop for a few seconds, making sure that he is watching you, then, with the customary exaggerated hand signal and verbal 'Get Out' or 'Go Back' send him for his unmarked retrieve. Now it should be obvious that the reason that several dummies were planted is to ensure a quick success. Upon a successful delivery the trainer may then elect to send the dog out for a second unseen dummy, as there are several dummies out there and success is very likely. Sending him for another retrieve is quite permissible but by no means mandatory. Upon receiving the second dummy, that finishes the lesson for that day, for four very good reasons. One, the trainer is pushing his luck, for, whenever he asks the dog to perform yet another retrieve, his chances of success diminish accordingly. Remember, rush nothing, make haste slowly, or you will pay the price. Two, the ground out there in the unmarked retrieve area is now becoming polluted by the dog's own scent where he has been questing, making success less likely for the dog to 'wind' another dummy. Three, never forget that retrieves should be kept to the minimum. Four, in asking overmuch of his dog, the trainer is defeating the purpose of this particular lesson, which is to build trust in the dog, which can only come from success.

I must emphasise that all lessons should be short and sweet. Five or six fifteen-minute lessons in a week are of far more value to the dog than a two hour session at the weekend. This lesson will in time be incorporated within the normal daily training regime, for it is an important one and is the precursor to a variety of more advanced training in retrieving exercises yet to come, such as 'the three ladies'.

As always, ensure that you end each lesson on a successful note by giving the dog an easy task to perform.

Chapter Twenty-Two

V

Videos

Shortly after *Training Spaniels* was published in 1980, I was approached by a burgeoning video company and asked if I would be interested in making a video pertaining to *Training Spaniels*. I think that I can fairly claim to be the first gundog trainer to have been approached with the making of a video in mind in the UK.

I replied and thanked them for their interest in me, but declined their offer. I refused then for the same reasons as I hold true to this day.

When it is considered that in a video, the dog can appear to have been trained to jump 'backward' over a gate, it must be clear that anything is possible. It is merely a matter of how many 'takes' are required until the desired effect is obtained. It is equally clear, with this in mind that the tapes can be so easily 'doctored' that the demands on the expertise of the handler are minimal.

As to value, I have grave doubts that there are many people who have bought a video tape and managed to train a dog by the sole use of it. I concede that the video tape may be of some use as an aid or a pointer as to what is required in a given movement or exercise contained in the tape. That said, in my opinion, the only claim that video tapes have is that they are of some assistance as a generalised guide to the training of a dog.

As I have said, I turned down the offer for I could see that there were opportunities for the video concept to be abused.

Voice

The use or lack of use of the voice in dog training is most important. I am sure that the significance of the voice, especially its effect on the dog, tends to escape the town dweller more so than those who spend their lives in the countryside and especially in the company of animals and the dog in particular.

Nevertheless, the fact that one spends most of their time in the company of dogs, sporting or otherwise, does not necessarily indicate a oneness with their animal counterpart. On the contrary, I have on many occasions found the incessant chatter put up by some dog handlers most irritating to the point of being unbearable.

Many aspiring dog handlers have asked the question, perhaps after I have demonstrated a particular dog or dogs, why, whilst I was paying attention to the client and thereby seemingly distracted, my dog's eyes were glued steadfastly on my face. It would be tempting to dismiss this nonchalantly by saying that it just happens that way, but that would be untrue. The answer is quite simply this. At all times when working with, or even in the company of your dog, you must only speak to him when it means something. Perhaps a small point, but an exceedingly important one.

Anyone who takes the trouble to examine the methods of a top-class dog handler will be struck by his economy with vocal commands. Moreover, at all times these vocal commands must be given in a low voice. Apart from the obvious fact that excessive noise will disturb game, the low voice and the paucity of commands demands complete attention from the dog.

As to tone of the given command, so long as it is consistently made in a low tone, the differing inflection made in the voice will be more than sufficient to signify to the dog the importance of the order. It can be seen therefore that there is no need, indeed it is undesirable for the voice to be raised except in an emergency, when the raised tone will command the dog's immediate attention to the fact that the handler is displeased.

If a secret there be in commanding undivided attention from a dog, then it is in the sparing use of commands by his handler.

Chapter Twenty-Three

W

Water – Introduction To (Intermediate & Advanced Training)

Thankfully, there are not many dogs who are genetically water-shy. Most working dogs love to swim. As with hard mouth and gun-shyness, water-shyness on the whole has been systematically bred out of the working breeds by the dedicated breeder down through the centuries. Nevertheless most professional trainers will, from time to time receive a young dog for training that is genetically water-shy.

The time of year that the dog is admitted to kennels for training can determine just how expensive the training will be. For, if the dog is brought into kennels during the winter, it could be many months into its training schedule before the fault of water-shyness is discovered. There is no professional trainer worth his salt who would risk attempting to enter a young dog to water during the cold months of winter, for fear of permanently averting him from it. Consequently, a pup brought in for training in early November could have at least three months' fees spent on his training before the fault is discovered. On the other hand, a pup brought in for training in April will be tested as to his or her attitude to water during its statutory assessment within its first month in training.

There are dogs who are water-shy, not through genetics but through stupidity. There are instances when, due to the ham-fisted methods employed by the 'trainer', a puppy has been abreacted from water for life. Believe it or not, there are owners who have been known to throw a three-month puppy into the water, just for curiosity, to see if it would swim! In my view, only a person mentally challenged would throw a pup into water and expect it to enjoy the experience. Moreover, it would not be at all surprising if that pup never faced water again. Even if a pup that had suffered a traumatic experience regarding its premature introduction to water and showed a marked reluctance to enter water, all is not necessarily lost. It is possible with extra work, which will cost the owner, that an understanding trainer may bring about a cure. If the fault is through bad breeding, there is nothing that can be done about it. Nor can the professional trainer be faulted for not discovering that the dog was water-shy sooner if the pup was brought in for training during the winter months.

Advice

The trainer would be wise to choose the area within which he intends to initiate the young dog's introduction to water very carefully. Avoid an area of water with steep banks which may prove difficult for the dog to get out of. If it is flowing water as in a river or stream, try to choose an area where the current is slow moving, for there are occasions when a pup just cannot understand the movement on his body from the river's current, thereby increasing his lack of confidence in this new environment. Swift-moving currents are most definitely not the ideal venue from where to encourage a young dog to swim. Dogs, like people, vary greatly and whilst many pups, even those who turned out to be excellent swimmers, needed encouragement, there were the occasional dogs where fear just did not exist.

Approximately two hundred metres from my kennels was the 'Blue Eel Pool', which derived its name from its cobalt shade of water. I never used this pool for novices, for there was a four-metre waterfall that tumbled straight down into the deep swift water of the pool, but all my seasoned dogs visited this pool due to its closeness to the kennels. On a hot day I would take a group of experienced water dogs down to the pool where I knew they would enjoy jumping into the swift water to be borne downstream until the current slackened when they would then swim to the bank and come scrambling up the bank to take leaps once more into the pool, having the time of their lives. The first time that I took Macsiccar Merrit, 'Merry', in the company of a few others down to the pool, imagine my horror on looking up at the waterfall to see her standing on a rock, obviously contemplating taking the leap into the falls. I called her and whistled at her, but it was useless. She could not hear me for the thunderous noise. She leapt into the falls and immediately disappeared in the frothing torrent to reappear bobbing in the swift current at the bottom of the falls and was swept down to the slower eddies. Relieved upon seeing her safe, I thought, well madam, I bet that has taught you a lesson, you won't do that again in a hurry. No sooner had the thought passed through my mind than she came hurtling past me going full-steam ahead, up the rocks and with no hesitation this time took a flying leap straight out into the middle of the falls to repeat the performance once more. Every time thereafter at the pool her favourite escapade was the waterfall.

I favour a pond with gravel around its edges, where the depth of water slowly shelves deeper into the middle. In such a venue the trainer's work is simplified greatly, for whilst many pups of a bolder character will charge straight into water as though they had been doing so all of their lives, the more timorous pup will hesitate and run up and down the water's edge. More often than not, such a pup, obviously jealous of his kennel mates having such a good time, will rush up and down in the shallow water, gradually getting deeper as his confidence grows until eventually his paws leave the bed of the pond. It does not matter if on the first or second outing the pup does not actually swim, it is enough that he is losing his fear of this new element. In all probability in due course he will enter and swim freely.

The successful dog trainer is the one most capable of looking at the world through the dog's eyes and acting accordingly. Water with a ripple upon it can be quite puzzling to a novice dog, even quite frightening, for if the trainer takes into consideration the dog's lack of imagination and limited reasoning powers, he will be aware, that to a young pup movement signifies life and he is instinctively afraid of the unknown. The introduction to water for the first time for a young dog is the only time that I would concede that the older dog acting as the 'schoolmaster' is of an advantage, then again, if the trainer is the owner of the pup's mother, this is an ideal setting within which to encourage the pup to follow his mother into the water. Initially, the trainer will take a number of dogs to the water. The middle of a heatwave, when any training except in the early morning or in the evening, was impossible, was the time that I would utilise giving the dogs a swim.

At no time must the novice swimmer be forced to enter the water, but close observation of his attitude to the water as he watches the other dogs enthusiastically swimming will indicate to the trainer what course of action to adopt. If after he has been watching the 'schoolmaster' dogs for a little time, he is running up and down the water's edge obviously wishing to join them but unsure of himself, try gently cajoling him to enter. If he still refuses, then call it a day.

A pup that turns and runs as soon as it sees the water is either genetically water-shy or it has had a traumatic experience in relation to water. There is only one way to find out. If after a few outings to the water and watching the other dogs swimming, and all the coaxing has failed and he is still refusing to take the plunge, so to speak, then as a last ditch attempt before informing his owner of the bad news, I would play my last card and, if it failed, then the dog had failed in his training.

I would put on my fishing waders and take the dog alone to the pond. With a check cord attached to him (yes, I admit that occasionally they have their uses) I would let him run up and down at the water's edge, whilst I wandered nonchalantly up and down in the pond. On many occasions I found that this was sufficient encouragement for him to gambol deeper into the water of his own accord. However, if he showed that he was still unwilling to chance his luck in this new environment, as a last resort, I would tighten up on the check cord and gradually and gently try to pull him into the shallows. If it appeared that he was becoming distressed at this approach, I would not pursue it further. Returning to the gravel bank, I would settle him down by gently stroking him and making soothing noises. As soon as it was apparent that all was well again, with one hand on the cord and the other beneath his chin, I would slowly take him gently out into the water until his paws lost contact with the bed of the pond and, supporting him under the chin keeping his mouth and nostrils clear of the water surface, I would walk him up and down the pond for a few minutes. I have found that in ninety per cent of cases where a pupil was afraid of water, this treatment was highly successful.

Water – Retrieving From (Intermediate & Advanced Training)

Once the dog has become thoroughly at ease with water, is a bold and confident swimmer and is efficient in retrieving on land, then retrieving from water should present no problems.

Simply sit him down on the bank and give him a marked retrieve on the water, but not too far for the first few times; remember the trainer must always load the dice in his own favour and therefore ensure success with the early retrieving from water. Making sure that there is a suitable pause, then give him the command that you would normally give to the dog when asked to retrieve from land, i.e. 'Dead There – Get Out – Get Out!' Never send him more than once on the same day. Remember commonsense, is to be recommended in all exercises involving retrieving. However, in an effort to ring the changes, one retrieve from land that day would be quite permissible.

Later, just as on land, variety can be introduced with the water retrieving also. For instance, one in the water and one on the far bank. Again, as with the first few dummies in the water, the trainer must ensure that the first few times a dummy is launched on the the far bank they are marked by the dog, therefore making it easy for him. It is also wise to select a spot where the far bank does not require a long swim for the dog. The trainer may now feel confident enough to try one in the water and one unmarked on the bank or vice versa.

As his confidence grows with his experience in water, you should be able to handle him with whistles and hand signals exactly as you would on land and to any retrieve that circumstance may put your way.

Once you are satisfied with the dog's prowess with the marked dummy on the far bank and the one in the water, it will be time to try a further deviation to the scheme, which is similar to 'The Three Ladies' retrieving on land. Initially, all three dummies, two in water and one on land, will be marked. Then perhaps, two on land marked and one in the water also marked. Remembering that it takes time, and this is not a race, we progress to two dummies marked and one unmarked and thereafter the trainer can mix and match the routine.

Whistles

There is a staggering choice of whistles available these days. I believe the gundog accessories manufacturers, Turner Richards, from whom I purchased all my equipment, have in the region of twenty-eight different types.

Each to our individual tastes and I have no wish to influence anyone, for each of us has our likes and dislikes. I have already stated my reasons for distrusting the 'silent' whistle regarding variance of tone.

Through experience I arrived at my personal preferences. I did not like the metal type of whistle because on a frosty morning it tended to adhere to my lips which could be painful, therefore I have always preferred the plastic whistle.

As my experience grew, I realised that the utilisation of one whistle for all commands which many gundog trainers seem to like, had its drawbacks. I noticed that there were times when the unavoidable similarities between certain commands uttered from the same whistle tended to confuse the dog, albeit in many instances only momentarily. But as a professional I was compelled to show my expertise in the field trial shop window and even if the dog's confusion might only result in a partial hesitation, those few seconds were crucial time that I could ill afford to lose. Therefore, I reasoned that to avoid any chance of confusion in my dogs, the two whistles that I used would need to be of a vastly different tone.

My ultimate choice of whistles which through the years have served me well, consisted of a set of two, both of which are readily available from my old suppliers – the 'Acme Thunderer' and the number 210 (without the pea). The loud distinctive 'chirp-like' tone of the 'Thunderer' is completely unmistakable in contrast to the sharper 'peep' of the 210.

As with all signals, hand, voice or whistle, they are intended merely as a guide to the dog and must not be overdone, for too many voice or whistle

Types of whistle.

commands will tend to alert game of your presence and will certainly minimise your chances of success in a field trial. Also a proliferation of signals are unnecessary and tend to confuse the dog instead of guiding it.

The handler who is forever nagging the dog with a profusion of commands, whether by voice, whistle, hand or a combination of all, will in time inadvertently teach the dog to ignore him. The trainer must therefore school himself to minimalise all commands, so when given an order, it will register as important to the dog and thereby increase his ability to obey.

The duration of the whistle signal is also crucial, for if prolonged, in time it will convey the impression to the dog that there is ample time to react to it. A lazy response is thereby cultivated.

A note of urgency must always be the rule of the day. Any signal uttered must mean now, not when it suits the dog. To achieve this all signals must be brief, only short and sharp will engender a short and sharp response.

The 'Thunderer' is used for only one command, short and sharp. It means 'STOP' and it means now, thereby it conveys maximum importance and there is no excuse. There can be no confusion.

The 210 plastic pea-less whistle is used for two responses, but as always is uttered in short sharp peeps to command obedience 'Now!' The single 'peep' is used to turn the dog from left to right or vice versa. The double 'peep – peep' is used to bring the dog back to hand or in conjunction with the single 'peep' to pull him back if he is threatening to hunt out of shot. It is also important that a suitable interval between the individual signals is allowed in order not to confuse the dog.

(*see* Dashing along the Hedgerows, page 25; Directing the 'turn', page 27; Drop – Disobedience to, page 33; Disobeying the 'Return' Whistle, page 31)

Wind – Cheek Treatment (Intermediate & Advanced Training)

Directional wind treatment in relation to retrieving from water is not something that a trainer can teach a dog to treat properly, for providing that the dog has efficient marking powers aided by a good sense of smell in approaching his target, he will adapt to water retrieving accordingly.

In giving guidance to the dog in water to the cheek wind situation, on telling him to 'Get In', the handler will allow the dog to accept directions as he would in ground treatment exercises and once again, similarly to ground treatment, when the handler considers the dog to be at a comfortable distance, he will turn him with the single 'peep' of the plastic pea-less turn whistle in conjunction with the appropriate hand signal toward the floating or unmarked dummy on the land. The trainers who train a multitude of dogs will in time be able to compare several dogs' widely different reactions in respect to wind treatment on land as well as water, which will be, as with many aspects of their environment, widely varied.

If a dog has poor marking ability or is somewhat deficient in scenting powers, there is little if anything that can be done with such a dog, for as I have said many times, the best trainer in the world cannot give a dog talents that he does not possess already.

Wind – Down Treatment (Intermediate & Advanced Training)

I am firmly of the belief that a dog that has reached a high standard of efficiency in ground treatment on land under conventional conditions, i.e. the upwind or the cheek wind beat, will adapt quite rapidly with the minimum guidance from his trainer once he is introduced to working in the water to the downwind beat.

Chapter Twenty-Four

Y

Yapping – Yipping – Giving Tongue

Yipping – giving tongue; this is a most undesirable tendency in the gundog. It is not difficult to realise why this should be. In the normal shooting day situation, a noisy dog will alert and forewarn the game of the approaching guns to the extent that the gun is deprived of the shot. In the field trial situation, the dog that gives tongue is the kiss of death for his handler is disqualified out of hand and rightly so. When considering that generally speaking, the winning trial dog is classed as the dog most likely to fill the bag, then the dog that gives tongue could be relegated to the dog least likely!

An interesting point arises here however in relation to the degree of noise that is considered sufficient to disturb the game on the shooting day or to legitimately warrant disqualification during a field trial. I have, and I'm sure that many of my field trial contemporaries have also suffered by being disqualified because our dogs had made the slightest of squeaks or the merest of whimpers, either whilst hunting or waiting to be sent to retrieve. I have even been disqualified because the dog gave a yelp of pain having run into the sharp end of a broken branch whilst hunting in thick cover. It really comes down to the ability or willingness of the judge to exercise his or her unbiased discretion.

It can be fairly said that for our purposes in the shooting field, 'yipping' is a most undesirable trait and one to be discouraged. It is most common in the more excitable dog. There are those who do not think that giving tongue is genetically inherited but is induced by circumstance and the owner's demeanour in the dog's earlier training. For instance, it is possible with the more excitable dog that if upon being sent to retrieve the dummy and perhaps reluctant to come into hand for whatever reason, the handler becomes increasingly more enthusiastic in his attempt to encourage his dog and finally appears to the dog to be excited in praising him and thereby inducing the dog to become over-excited itself and perhaps begin to squeak.

Similarly, there are instances when giving tongue can be considered desirable and is deliberately encouraged by the owner in order to make visitors aware of the presence of a dog in the house to deter burglars for instance, simply by pointing towards the knocking on the door and excitedly in a raised stage whisper repeatedly enquiring of him, 'What is it? What is it?' If this behaviour is repeated every time the doorbell rings or knocking is heard, in a very short time indeed you will find that the dog will spring to its feet and start barking even a few seconds before the knocking is heard at the door. Ergo, you have conditioned the dog by your demeanour to react to the activity at the door. In this case it would seem the view that giving tongue is not genetically inherited but is acquired by the dog would initially appear to hold true. Without doubt there are many instances that prove that giving tongue can be induced, for instance, by introducing the dog to shooting far too early in its life. That in no way can rule out the case for genetic inheritance, for there is more than a concrete case to support the theory. Any trait induced by the handler can be eradicated whereas any genetically inherited trait is incurable, and furthermore the root cause can be recognised and traced back through the generations by the knowledgeable breeder. Take for example the case of the Aberdeenshire dog. I and my contemporaries inherited his progeny, a fair number of which were turned down by me because at six months old they were already in the embryonic stages of giving tongue. I also learned from other professionals, that having managed to train one or two of the progeny they found that as soon as they were introduced to the

Retrieving game – a Labrador with grouse.

exciting world of shooting for the first time they began to squeak.

I have to say that I do not think it wholly just to decry the fault of 'giving tongue'. In my view such could be termed an 'honest' fault, for it is in the surge of extreme effort upon winding and recognising the ever-increasing intense scent of the game and in the excitement of the moment that it occurs. This is an essential part of the make-up of our gundogs. Without the excitement engendered and induced by the chase, in the absence of such enthusiasm, effortless drive or the will to work for us enthusiastically and tirelessly, what kind of gundog would we end up with? A pretty dull and useless article, I venture to suggest. That is not to say that I condone the fault, merely that we cut a fine line between the desirable drive and enthusiasm so necessary in our gundogs and the undesirable in giving tongue.

Advice

I have to say that as a professional trainer I just simply did not have the time to devote to such a labour-intensive regime as curing such faults. Moreover I repeat, if the fault is genetical, it is therefore incurable. There are those who suggest that to cure the induced fault, it is simply a matter of keeping a rolled-up newspaper handy and whenever the dog squeaks, giving him a crack across the muzzle with the paper accompanied by a sharp 'No!' I hasten to add, this is not painful to the dog. It is more that the noise made by the paper hopefully discourages him from repeating the offence. I have heard that using a soda syphon is also useful by giving the dog a squirt whenever it gave tongue. I have never gone shooting with a rolled up newspaper at the ready nor have I ever pursued a spaniel through the thick cover with a soda syphon and, if I did, I would be fearful that my shooting companions might truss me up in a wraparound waistcoat! Obviously then, these remedies are suggested in treating the gundog puppy or young dog in his preshooting days. If you have a dog that gives tongue my advice would have to be, either put up with it or cut your losses and get yourself another dog.